The history, theology and ide us in a lively, readable manner itself, informs the mind and st 140 years without succumbing future that sees a new generation embracing the core convictions of 'the movement'.

CH00330558

Here is an explanation of evangelical unity (All One In Christ Jesus) that begins with people gathered under God's Word and united in God's work. It is both helpful and necessary for us to be reminded of the priority of God's Word, the necessity of God's Spirit, the unity of God's people, and the responsibility of God's mission for the world.

Readers in the USA will benefit particularly from the way in which common misunderstandings about Keswick are helpfully and graciously corrected. This book not only enables us to learn more about Keswick, but ultimately to Know God Better. Read it to your profit!

Rev Alistair Begg is Senior Pastor, Parkside Church, Cleveland USA, and an author and broadcaster.

'I'll tell you what your real problem is . . .' But I thought I knew. I was feeling rather 'weary and worn and sad' after a demanding first year in local church ministry, wondering if it might be time to quit. I can still hear Alec Motyer's penetrative diagnosis about my 'problem', as he expounded Nehemiah: 'You've lost your vision of God!' An arrow to my heart! A fresh meeting with the Lord through his Word. The road to recovery had appeared!

I know my experience of encountering and re-encountering the Living God at Keswick nearly forty years ago is not unique. It has been replicated many times as countless tens of thousands of believers over the 140-year history of the Convention have met the Lord. How does that happen? By some neat formula or special technique? No. But there are principles. In the pages of this fine book, you will discover many of them elegantly set out, biblically argued, and judiciously illustrated from Keswick's beginnings to the present day.

If you want to know what makes Keswick 'Keswick', here are its core convictions. And may you find your heart freshly warmed to Christ, and your vision of God increased by the work of his gracious Spirit.

Dr Steve Brady, Principal of Moorlands College and Trustee at Keswick Ministries

Knowing God Better is a great introduction to the history and passion of the Keswick movement. Along the way it corrects some of the misunderstandings still associated with the Convention, but *Knowing God Better* is more than this. It's an invitation to pursue God more, to know him better and to serve him fully. Inspirational stories and clear Bible exposition combine to give us a compelling picture of the Christian life, a life in which we are always receiving from God and always giving to the world in Christ's name. It's a call to a Christlike life lived in dependence on the Holy Spirit. I warmly encourage you to read this book and know God better.

Tim Chester, Director of Porterbrook Seminary and pastor of The Crowded House, Sheffield

Reading this short book has warmed my heart! It is so much more than an honest and open review of 140 years of the ministry of the Keswick Convention. That in itself is of great interest because of the significant global impact of this annual Bible convention. It is of personal interest to me since the Convention has played an enormous part in my spiritual formation from my early teenage years right up to the present.

However, what has thrilled me the most is the way the priorities and themes of the Keswick Convention have been explained and expounded. This book contains an inspiring reminder of Biblical principles that should be in the heart of every disciple of Jesus Christ. May many be helped along in their journey through life with the Lord Jesus by committing ourselves afresh to these great Bible truths – and may God the Father, Son and Holy Spirit, receive the glory!

Elaine Duncan, CEO, Scottish Bible Society

There are few conventions in the world that have had such a uniformly positive and powerful impact for the kingdom. The

Keswick Convention has modelled responsible and effective expository preaching and Bible study; has consistently made the plain things of Scripture the main things; has encouraged true unity around the Word of God among Christian people of all backgrounds; and has launched many into Christian work at home and around the world.

One of its many strengths is the expectation that, as we come together, God will – by his Word and Spirit – speak to the hearts and minds of his people. Though the Convention is not a church, it has been an oasis in the desert for many of God's people, providing much needed spiritual nourishment and encouragement to go back and serve sacrificially in small corners of the Master's vineyard. *Knowing God Better* is a heart-warming and soul-stirring introduction to a ministry and movement that seeks to bring glory to God by serving the church.
Liam Goligher, Senior Minister, Tenth Presbyterian Church, Philadelphia, USA

As Keswick celebrates its 140th birthday, this book gives a short, clear and warm insight into what forms the DNA of the Keswick movement. With its Christ-centred, Bible-based and Spirit-empowered preaching, Keswick has been used by God to bring countless blessings to his global church. The purpose of such preaching has always been to promote a passion for God, a longing for holiness, a desire for unity and a call to mission. The book highlights key speakers and vital moments in Keswick history, like the influence of the Welsh Revival in 1904 or Watchman Nee's prayer at the time of the Japanese invasion of China in 1938. It helpfully tackles some controversial areas such as teaching on holiness or the ministry of the Spirit. This book is an excellent description of where, under the good hand of the living God, Keswick has come from. It is also a brilliant platform for its future development. Reading this book will not only give you an insight into what makes Keswick tick, it will also challenge your passion for God and your commitment to his mission in the world. It is highly recommended.
Paul Mallard, pastor of Widcombe Baptist Church, Bath.

As a young man, I went to live and work in Zimbabwe for two years. On my first Sunday afternoon there, I listened to a reel-to-reel recording of John Stott speaking at the Keswick Convention in England. This was my first exposure to Keswick. This 'Keswick Fellowship', out in rural Africa, met every Sunday afternoon, and the Keswick speakers of that era became very familiar to me and their teaching profoundly influenced my understanding and experience of the Christian life.

Few movements have had a greater impact on the spiritual life of the entire twentieth century than the Keswick movement, not only in Great Britain, but in many parts of the world.

This book is historical and doctrinal, informative and challenging. The longevity of Keswick can be accounted for by its foundation – the Word of God; its subject – the Lord Jesus Christ as the source of all true Christian experience; and its object – holiness of life expressed in fruitful service.

Charles Price, Teaching Pastor, The Peoples Church, Toronto, Canada

Knowing God Better

The Vision of the Keswick Movement

Jonathan Lamb

with Ian Randall

KESWICK MINISTRIES
Keswick Convention Centre, Skiddaw Street, Keswick CA12 4BY
Email: info@keswickministries.org
Website: www.keswickministires.org

First published 2015

British Library Cataloguing in Publication Data
A catalogue record for this book is available from the British Library.

UK ISBN 978-1-78359-369-9

Set in Dante 12/15pt
Typeset in Great Britain by CRB Associates, Potterhanworth, Lincolnshire
Printed and bound in Great Britain by Ashford Colour Press Ltd, Gosport, Hampshire

Keswick Ministries is committed to the spiritual renewal of God's people for his mission in the world. For 140 years the work of Keswick has impacted churches worldwide.

Keswick Ministries is committed to strengthening its network in the UK and beyond, through prayer, news, pioneering and cooperative activity. In addition to its three-week Convention held in the town of Keswick, which attracts some 15,000 Christians, Keswick is producing a growing range of literature based on the core foundations of Christian life and mission.

Contents

Preface

It's a remarkable story. It spans 140 years and crosses cultures and continents. It has revolutionized hundreds of thousands of lives. It has had a radical impact on churches and communities. It has launched new mission movements and pushed forward the frontiers of the gospel. And it continues to expand, not through formal organization or slick marketing but, as we who are involved believe, as a movement of the Holy Spirit.

The Keswick movement has at its heart a commitment to the spiritual renewal of God's people for his mission in the world. Launched on the vicarage lawn of a small church in a small town 140 years ago, the Keswick movement arose from a longing to know God better. We believe that the priorities of that movement, which are addressed in the chapters that follow, represent vital commitments for every Christian believer, as well as central ingredients of the life of churches the world over. They can be summarized in the form of three fundamental convictions, which still shape the movement today.

First, hearing God's Word: the Scriptures are the foundation of the church's life, growth and mission, and *Keswick Ministries* is committed to the preaching and teaching of God's Word in a way that is faithful to Scripture and relevant to Christians of all ages and backgrounds.

Second, becoming like God's Son: from its earliest days, the Keswick movement has encouraged Christians to live godly lives in the power of the Spirit, to grow in Christlikeness and to live under his Lordship in every area of life. This is God's will for his people in every culture and generation.

Third, serving God's mission: the authentic response to God's Word is obedience to his mission, and the inevitable result of Christlikeness is sacrificial service. *Keswick Ministries* seeks to encourage committed discipleship in family life, work and society, and energetic engagement in the cause of world mission.

As we celebrate the 140th anniversary of the Keswick movement, we have highlighted the priorities that continue to shape its ministry, and have included in each chapter some historical sketches of how God has been at work over the years. I would like to express warm gratitude to Dr Ian Randall, the historian of the Keswick movement, for his insightful historical contributions to each chapter. A fuller account of the Keswick history was published by Dr Randall (with Charles Price) in *Transforming Keswick*, an excellent overview of the key historical issues.[1]

This short title includes some historical background, but is primarily intended to introduce the big themes that shape the worldwide movement, and that we believe are essential for today's church too. (An accompanying DVD set, *Knowing God Better*, is also available, with addresses that match some of the themes of this book, given by John Stott, Charles Price, Paul Mallard, Ajith Fernando and Jonathan Lamb, available from Essential Christian: https://www.essentialchristian.com/keswick-convention). We hope that this small book will contribute to the spiritual renewal of God's people for his mission in the world, encouraging every reader to pursue Christlikeness for his greater glory.

Jonathan lamb

1

Longing for God's blessing

Mountaineering is a risky business. On Mont Blanc alone, the death toll is well over one hundred a year. In a recent radio programme, Sandi Toksvig asked three mountaineers why they risked life and limb in such a dangerous pursuit, and they each replied that they were enchanted by the goal – the summit. The unspeakable beauty of the mountains more than compensated for the costs that they incurred. One of the mountaineers quoted the example of the climber Herzog, who wrote a book on his exploits. Well, he didn't write it, he dictated it – he had lost all his fingers through frostbite. The summit was more important than fingers and toes.

It doesn't seem adequate to call it a hobby, does it? Their lives were dominated by an all-consuming passion and purpose. It stands in stark contrast to how many people live their lives today. The actress Helena Bonham Carter summed up the popular view: 'We're all going to die anyway; so what does it matter so long as you keep a sense of humour and have fun?' But you don't have to be a sophisticated social commentator to recognize that most people are looking for a deeper

meaning, a higher purpose, and there frequently comes a
point when they recognize that, for all their self-indulgence,
they are deeply dissatisfied.

What are we made for? What is the purpose of our lives?
What is it that motivates us, that shapes our decisions and
determines our priorities? What really matters? The biblical
answer is found in a lovely prayer which was the focus of the
apostle Paul's concern not just for the Ephesian Christians,
but for every Christian believer:

> I keep asking that the God of our Lord Jesus Christ, the
> glorious Father, may give you the Spirit of wisdom and
> revelation, so that you may know him better.
> (Ephesians 1:17)

That is the purpose of life: to know the God of the universe,
to know the God who has made us and who loves us, to know
him personally and to know him deeply. The prophet Jeremiah
exposed the folly of imagining
that the purpose of life is to do
with such things as human
power, or wealth or learning.
He spoke the incisive Word
of the Lord: 'Let not the wise
boast of their wisdom or the
strong boast of their strength
or the rich boast of their riches,
but let the one who boasts boast

*That is the purpose of
life: to know the God
of the universe . . . to
know him personally
and to know him
deeply.*

about this: that they have the understanding to know me'
(Jeremiah 9:23–24).

That's what really matters: to know God better. Paul begins
the section in Ephesians 1 with the phrase *'For this reason'*,
because he has previously been thanking God for all of the

rich blessings in Christ that belong to those who know God. He had been praying that we would truly grasp these blessings, allowing them to shape the whole of life.

But, if we are honest, we know our hearts. We know that there is a constant drift away from a true devotion to the God who made us and loved us. We are surrounded by the distractions of a world that disowns God. Our sinful hearts are so often indifferent, seeking fulfilment elsewhere. That's why Paul continues to pray that the Holy Spirit will open our hearts and eyes and ears and minds (v. 18), so that we truly know God and experience his power in our lives (v. 19). In fact, when Jesus declared his manifesto of the kingdom, it was here that he began. As he introduced the priorities of his rule and explained how men and women might know God's blessing, his very first statement was: 'Blessed are those who know their need of God' (Matthew 5:3, NEB).

Hungry for God

Today, many Christians long for a deeper understanding and experience of God; we are hungry for the reality of God. We realize it is the most important thing of all. Don Carson, a regular speaker at Keswick, has expressed it like this: 'The one thing we most urgently need in Western Christendom is a deeper knowledge of God. We need to know God better. When it comes to knowing God we are a culture of the spiritually stunted. So much of our religion is packaged to address our felt needs – and these are almost uniformly anchored in our pursuit of our own happiness and fulfilment . . . We are not captivated by his holiness and his love; his thoughts and words capture too little of our imagination, too little of our discourse, too few of our priorities.'[1]

A longing for God's blessing has been the foundation of the work and growth of the Keswick movement all around the world. It has been driven by the desire for a true encounter with the living God, by a longing for the renewal of spiritual life – personally, corporately and even nationally. And in towns and cities around the world, in small home groups or conventions numbering hundreds of thousands, God's people have opened the Scriptures, entered God's presence, and sought his blessing.

At the time when the Keswick Convention began, many Christians were aware of personal spiritual need and of a longing for a deeper experience of God. There was great interest in the 1870s in the possibility of what was termed the 'higher Christian life', 'victory through faith' and 'deliverance from sin'. A number of key figures who spread this message came from North America, including Robert Pearsall Smith and his wife, Hannah Whitall Smith, but the Keswick Convention's early period owed more to a number of Anglican founding fathers. One of them was Evan Hopkins, who was the energetic vicar of Holy Trinity, Richmond in the later nineteenth century. In 1879 he was deeply affected as he heard Robert Pearsall Smith speak about spiritual power and, for Evan Hopkins, a new phase of spiritual experience began.[2] Pretty soon the services in Hopkins's church regularly concluded with an 'after-meeting', at which people were encouraged to go beyond their previous Christian experience and make a full consecration of their lives to Christ.[3] Within a year, others who shared this longing for God organized a two-day conference at St Jude's in north London 'for the promotion of spiritual life'. The parish church had become known for evangelical conferences, and this 1874 gathering was a forerunner of Keswick.

Drawing closer to God

Sometimes God can use difficulty, or even tragedy, to help us discover what really matters. There are mysteries here, but in God's redemptive purpose such events can help us depend on him, and come to know him better. There are many examples we could give. One of them is the story of another influential figure in the early days of the Keswick movement. H. W. Webb-Peploe served as the vicar of St Paul's, Onslow Square, in London for forty-three years. In 1874 he was on holiday with his wife and youngest child when a friend bluntly asked him: 'Have you got peace?' Three days after this challenge, Webb-Peploe suffered the crushing blow of the death of his six-month-old son. The scripture lesson assigned for the following Sunday, when he was due to preach in his own church, included the text 'My grace is sufficient for you'. In that moment of crisis he heard God telling him that, if he believed divine grace was sufficient for his needs, he would find that this was indeed the case.[4]

In fact, many of us know this experience. God takes us through a period of personal trial and, although it is often bewildering at the time, it can, as with Webb-Peploe, be the very means that God uses to draw us closer to himself.

But, away from London, in the beautiful Lake District town of Keswick, the person who was responsible for the first Convention was Thomas Dundas Harford-Battersby. As vicar of St John's Church in Keswick from 1851, he was active in community outreach and also attempted to mobilize Christians of different denominations to work together, a theme we'll take up in a later chapter. In 1873 he read a book by Hannah Whitall Smith, and he recorded in his diary that the book had 'made me utterly dissatisfied with myself . . . I must either go backwards or forwards'.[5] He attended meetings in Oxford in September 1874, and a talk given by Evan Hopkins had a profound impact on him. He later spoke of the Oxford meetings as 'a revelation of Christ' to his soul and, fired by this experience, he attended a convention at Brighton in the early summer of 1875. It was here that Harford-Battersby announced that three days of 'Union Meetings for the Promotion of Practical Holiness' would be held, from Tuesday 29 June 1875, in a tent in Keswick.

Waiting on God

Between three and four hundred attended this first Keswick meeting, and Harford-Battersby set the opening theme by speaking from Psalm 62:5: 'My soul, wait thou only upon God, for my expectation is from him (KJV).' There was a particular emphasis on the need and provision for cleansing from sin, and on resting in the sufficiency of Christ. The opening days of many subsequent Conventions also began with a time of self-examination, and such honest evaluation before the Lord is often a vital ingredient in discovering our need of Christ.

Two years later the numbers at the Convention had grown to 900. More important than the gradual numerical advance was the fact that the Convention was acquiring a reputation as a place of spiritual power. One publication spoke of nowhere being more suited than the Convention at Keswick for 'turning aside to learn more of the things of God'.[6] And so, by the end of the 1870s, a group of trusted Keswick speakers had emerged, determined to bring messages from Scripture that related to the deepening of spiritual experience. By the 1887 Convention there were 3,000 present, meeting in a large tent on the outskirts of town, with Keswick's guest houses and hotels filled with convention-goers.

And God was at work in other leaders too. There was Handley Moule, who eventually became Bishop of Durham. He came to inner transformation and renewal through hearing the persuasive teaching of Evan Hopkins. Moule had been opposed to Keswick teaching as he understood it, but at the same time he was aware of 'discreditable failures in patience, and charity, and humbleness' in his own ministry. In his experience of spiritual transformation, his longings for God and for authentic Christian living were truly satisfied. Speaking at Keswick some thirty-six years later, Moule gave an unusually intimate description of how he had first yielded fully to God. Another leader in the 1880s was F. B. Meyer, a well-known Baptist minister, whose contribution to the movement also grew from his experience of consecration to God and subsequent personal transformation.[7]

There were variations in the emphases of Keswick speakers, but they were united by their own longing for God and a desire to help to meet the wider longing among many Christians of their time: to discover the reality of God's life and the experience of his power, just as Paul had prayed for those Ephesian Christians (Ephesians 1:15–20). They experienced the need for honest self-evaluation in God's presence; the awareness of their own spiritual poverty; the horror at their own sinfulness; the longing for God's comforting presence and the power of his Spirit. They all wished to know God better. And, before we look at other features of this remarkable movement, it's important to pause for a moment and ask about our own spiritual longing.

Seeking God

Psalm 63 is a very personal song, and it uses language that we too might wish to employ: 'You, God, are my God, earnestly

I seek you; I thirst for you, my whole being longs for you, in a dry and parched land where there is no water' (v. 1). It's a graphic description of David's sense of need, descriptive not of a physical hunger or thirst, but of an inner hunger, a deep longing for God himself. Many Christians find that there are times when particular events or situations throw us off balance. Or we find that the deceitfulness of our hearts leads us away from a wholehearted devotion to the Lord. We begin to feel a spiritual barrenness. In some cases this leads to a more extreme sense of desolation, which the Puritans referred to as 'the dark night of the soul'. Psalm 42, like Psalm 63, begins with the image of a deer panting from thirst along some dry river bed, and it vividly expresses our sense of desperation.

One of the refreshing things about the psalmist is the complete honesty of the way in which he expresses himself. We've seen this in the experience of some of the founding leaders of the Keswick movement, and it is an important pre-requisite for experiencing God's blessing. There is no point in pretending, whether in front of God or in front of other Christians. As Jim Packer has expressed it in his book *Knowing God*, 'Unreality towards God is the wasting disease of much modern Christianity. We need God to make us realists both about ourselves and about God.'[8]

Do you remember when Jesus used the same imagery as the psalmists? There are a couple of occasions in John's Gospel. One was when he spoke with the Samaritan woman. Despite six love affairs, she lived in a relational desert. She had hoped that marriage would make her life worthwhile, but somehow every relationship had turned sour. And there, with her empty water pot, she stands as a symbol of how many of us feel. And Jesus breaks in to challenge the spiritual emptiness in her life. 'Everyone who drinks this water will be thirsty again, but whoever drinks the water I give them will never thirst. Indeed, the water I give them will become in them a spring of water welling up to eternal life' (John 4:13, 14). A little later in John's Gospel, on the last and greatest day of the festival, Jesus stood and said in a loud voice: 'Let anyone who is thirsty come to me and drink. Whoever believes in me, as Scripture has said, rivers of living water will flow from within them' (John 7:37, 38).

The prophet Isaiah called people to find their satisfaction in God alone. Why look elsewhere? 'Why spend money on what is not bread, and your labour on what does not satisfy?' (Isaiah 55:2). There is a certain tragedy in missing true satisfaction by being content with something less than God is offering. Jeremiah used a graphic image when he said that the Jewish people preferred the mirage to the true oasis of satisfaction: 'My people have committed two sins: they have forsaken me, the spring of living water, and have dug their own cisterns, broken cisterns that cannot hold water' (Jeremiah 2:13). In their context, that meant they were trying to gain some nourishment from the husks of pagan religion rather than coming to the banquet that God had provided for them. It's rather like the story of the prodigal son in Luke 15, wandering off to a far country to eat pigs' food, until he came to his senses and returned home, where his father had a party prepared.

Knowing Christ Jesus

What comes across in these different passages is something very fundamental. It is what Jesus said in Matthew 4:4: 'Man shall not live on bread alone, but on every word that comes from the mouth of God.' He is our life, he is our satisfaction, our joy. Everything else is secondary. And we are going to see in the chapters that follow that spiritual longings are met only in Jesus Christ. We know from Paul's testimony that something happened on the Damascus Road when he met Jesus. When he added up all his natural benefits and achievements, he discovered that they came to zero. 'But whatever were gains to me I now consider loss for the sake of Christ' (Philippians 3:7). His encounter with Christ spelt the death of his egocentric pretensions of worthiness, his confidence in the flesh: 'I consider everything a loss because of the surpassing worth of knowing Christ Jesus my Lord . . . I want to know Christ' (Philippians 3:8–10).

Paul had never known God in an intimate or personal way. No amount of moral effort or good behaviour or religious observance could provide him with the warmth and the joy of communion with God. But now Paul describes how he had come to 'know Christ Jesus my Lord'. And it was this fellowship with Christ that brought him something that confidence in the flesh never could – a restored relationship with God, a spiritual satisfaction, a peace of conscience, a freedom from guilt, true hope beyond the grave.

And this is why Paul prayed that prayer for the Ephesians, and why we too must seek the Lord's blessing. Let's take a moment to pray that same prayer, because nothing else matters more than this:

'I keep asking that the God of our Lord Jesus Christ, the glorious Father, may give you the Spirit of wisdom and revelation, so that you may know him better. I pray that the eyes of your heart may be enlightened in order that you may know the hope to which he has called you, the riches of his glorious inheritance in his holy people, and his incomparably great power for us who believe.'
(Ephesians 1:17–19)

2

Hearing God's Word

Working on a paraphrase of the Bible some years ago, the scholar–clergyman J. B. Phillips explained that the experience was similar to working on the mains electricity of a house, but doing so with the electricity still switched on! It was an extraordinary experience – the book was 'live'; it was powerful and energizing. As the sixteenth-century Reformer Martin Luther put it, 'The Bible is alive – it has hands and grabs hold of me, it has feet and runs after me.'

The Bible is full of dynamic descriptions of itself. Jeremiah said that God's Word was like fire in his bones, or like a hammer that breaks a rock in pieces. Paul described it as the sword of the Spirit. This idea is repeated in Hebrews 4: 'alive and active. Sharper than any double-edged sword'. Jesus said that the Word was the seed that produced a wonderful harvest. And there is the intriguing story in Luke 24, when two disciples were walking home to Emmaus after the dramatic events of Jesus' crucifixion in Jerusalem. They didn't recognize Jesus, but he deliberately chose not to reveal himself, other than through the Bible. 'And beginning with Moses and all the

Prophets, he explained to them what was said in all the Scriptures concerning himself.' So they said: 'Were not our hearts burning within us while he talked with us on the road and opened the Scriptures to us?'

In other words, it was through Scripture that they encountered the living Christ. This is the reason why local churches are committed to listening to, understanding and explaining God's Word, and why the Keswick movement continues to be focused on Scripture. It is because we believe God's Word has the same dynamic impact today. It transforms understanding and attitudes; it changes lives; it draws us into a living relationship with God.

In the last chapter I mentioned the vicar who launched Keswick on his front lawn, Thomas Harford-Battersby. He reported on the 1880 Convention with a simple but profound statement: 'Our prayer was for deep, clear, powerful teaching, which would take hold of the souls of the people, and overwhelm them, and lead them to a full, definite, and all-conquering faith in Jesus.'[1] In fact, this explains why hundreds of thousands of Christians the world over have been committed to the Keswick movement. The *purpose* is nothing other than to see believers more wholeheartedly committed to Jesus Christ in every area of life, and the *means* is the faithful, clear and relevant exposition of God's Word. All around the world the Keswick movement has this purpose and this means. Whether it is to encourage discipleship, to call for holiness, to urge for mission, to appeal for unity, to provoke life change, to long for the Spirit – expounding the Bible is central to fulfilling these priorities.

Why the stress on the Bible?

There's a clear answer from the story of a week-long Bible convention – let's call it the Jerusalem Convention, which is described in Nehemiah 8. God's people had returned home from exile and had begun to reconstruct the city's walls. But, once that task had been completed, there was a remarkable turning point in the reconstruction of their national life.

The foundation of God's Word

Their first act was to call for the book. Nehemiah describes the grassroots desire that the law should be read: 'all the people came together as one in the square before the Water Gate. They told Ezra the teacher of the law to bring out the Book of the Law of Moses, which the Lord had commanded for Israel' (Nehemiah 8:1). And everyone listened carefully (v. 3), because the Word of God represented the foundation articles, the new constitution, of the people of God.

Why was this important? It was because the law was from God himself. They told Ezra to bring out the Book of the Law of Moses, 'which the LORD had commanded for Israel'. Yes, it was recorded by Moses, but its divine authority is emphasized. It was the law of God, the revelation given by him. The law was 'teaching' or instruction from God himself. That's why we too must take God's Word seriously. There is a wonderful explanation of this in 1 Thesssalonians, as Paul describes how the believers welcomed the apostolic message: 'We also thank God continually because, when you received the word of God, which you heard from us, you accepted it not as a human word, but as it actually is, the word of God, which is indeed at work in you who believe' (1 Thesssalonians 2:13).

First, the Word of God is authoritative. We must accept it 'as it actually is – the word *of God*'. This is strongly emphasized in the way that Paul wrote it. The message of the apostles is authoritative because it originates with God himself. And so it is powerful: 'the word of God, which is indeed at work in you who believe'. By God's Spirit it is life-giving and life-transforming. It goes on working in those who go on believing. As Luther said: 'I just threw the Bible into the congregation and the word did the work.' So Paul thanks God that the Thessalonian believers 'accepted it' as God's Word. They heard it, but they also welcomed it in as a friend; it became part of them, continuing its work in their lives.

What a great example of God's transforming Word. It is not simply cold propositions, but a dynamic message that, by the power of the Spirit, turns us round to serve God, and shapes the way in which we are to live. And that's why Ezra and Nehemiah were so concerned that everyone should understand what was being read. If God's Word was to be the foundation for their families, their day-to-day living, their relationships and even their economic activity, then it had to be clear and accessible to everyone.

For one thing, everyone was present: 'all the people came together as one' (v. 1); Ezra read before the assembly, 'which was made up of men and women and all who were able to understand' (vv. 2, 3); then 'all the people could see him' (v. 5). But not only that: 'everyone understood', because they worked hard to make the content of the law clear, 'giving the meaning so that the people could understand what was being read' (v. 8). The reason for the people's response is 'because they now understood the words that had been made known to them' (v. 12). They used teams of helpers, working in small groups to translate the message into local dialects or to explain what God's Word meant. What comes across clearly is the need to make the book accessible to all.

Clear and plain

Throughout its history, the Keswick movement has sought to ensure that God's Word is central and accessible. In 1881, six years after Keswick started, expository Bible readings were introduced, and these have remained a notable feature of the Convention. The term 'Bible reading' describes a teaching style that works steadily through a Bible book or sequence of Bible passages, and 'exposition' simply means making God's Word clear and plain. It is to bring out what is there. Exposition is sometimes caricatured as though it is simply a running commentary on a lengthy passage, for example, taking four years of Sundays to preach through the whole of Leviticus! Or perhaps we think it is a particular cultural style with three neat points held together by 'apt alliterations' artful aid'. But exposition is opening up a Bible passage in order to expose its force and power.

The very first Keswick Bible Readings were conducted compellingly by Hubert Brooke, who was a vicar in Reading, and he became well known for the promotion of biblical exposition in the wider Keswick movement. The Keswick emphasis began to spread widely. For example, in 1893 three Keswick speakers, one of them Hubert Brooke and the other two George Macgregor, from Scotland, and Charles Inwood, a Methodist minister from Ireland, undertook a three-month tour of Canada to speak about the Keswick message. It was reckoned that in the meetings they conducted Brooke brought 'exposition', Macgregor contributed 'argument', and Inwood produced 'arousement'. But Webb-Peploe was probably the preacher who became best known for his powerful biblical exposition at Keswick in the Convention's early decades. His style was commanding, perhaps somewhat autocratic, yet his messages were invariably full of instruction and inspiration for Keswick-goers. He gave detailed scriptural expositions without the use of notes, and between 1893 and 1921 Webb-Peploe was a speaker at almost every Keswick Convention.[2]

John Stott, who was a remarkable global evangelical leader and an influential Keswick speaker from the 1960s onwards, often underlined that all true Christian preaching is expository preaching, in the broad sense that it opens up the biblical text: 'In expository preaching, the biblical text is neither a conventional introduction to a sermon on a largely different theme, nor a convenient peg on which to hang a ragbag of miscellaneous thoughts, but a master which dictates and controls what is said.'[3]

Our conviction is that Scripture is the authoritative and powerful Word of God and that, if the Bible is God's Word, his voice must be heard. So our attitude must be to submit to God's Word, committed above all to letting the Bible do the talking. In that sense, Bible exposition is not so much a method as a mindset: our attitude is one of submission to that Word, ensuring that what is preached flows directly from that divine revelation.[4]

The Bible speaks

Over the years, speakers have come to Keswick from varying theological backgrounds, whether Free Church or Anglican, Reformed or Charismatic, but all with the same desire to allow the Scriptures to speak. Donald Grey Barnhouse spoke in the 1940s, and came from a Reformed background. He was a Presbyterian minister from Philadelphia, USA and, in 1959, he made a significant observation about the way biblical material was handled at Keswick. He stated: 'A theologian who has followed the reports of the past three-quarters of a century would quickly recognize that many phases of the doctrine of holiness have been presented by a wide variety of speakers, some of them contradictory. Keswick teaching certainly does not have the "party line" spirit, which is extremely important as the Holy Spirit does not express Himself in rigid legalistic forms.'[5] The concern of the Convention has been that the first priority for speakers is that they should wrestle with and apply the biblical text. Keswick speakers have sought to expound the Scripture as it stands – or at least, that has been the aim. That is why the Bible expositions at each Keswick week, working faithfully through Bible books or passages, have formed the backbone of the Convention.

John Stott had a great impact when he gave the morning Bible teaching at Keswick. As we have noted, he was known worldwide as an evangelical leader, and was particularly appreciated as an outstanding Bible teacher and writer. Whenever he spoke his addresses were invariably marked by lucidity and depth. At the 1962 Convention, the report in *The Keswick Week* stated that the main characteristic of the meetings that year was exposition of Scripture, directed more to the mind and will than to the emotions (though at Keswick the variety of speakers invariably results in a rounded mix of preaching styles). Stott's Bible readings were regarded as masterly. These set the tone and were seen by some as ranking among the great utterances delivered at Keswick, and many of these addresses found their way into print and into multiple languages.

The emphasis on clear and relevant Bible teaching has been sustained at Keswick throughout the years, and this is vital today because many Christians no longer know the Bible, or understand the significance of Bible books – and, even less, the story line of the Bible as a whole. The life, health and mission of the churches depends on a return to biblical literacy. And, just as in the account in Nehemiah 8, not only must the Bible remain central in the Keswick movement, it must also be accessible. This always demands creative effort, as we teach the truth of God's Word to children of all ages, as we apply God's Word to young people growing up in an increasingly secular culture, and as we make it available on all kinds of platforms, whether MP3, DVD, radio or TV. We must make the Word accessible to as wide an audience as possible.

The hunger of God's people

Back at the Jerusalem Convention (Nehemiah 8), the people were eager to hear the message. This too is an essential ingredient in being transformed by the power of God's Word and Spirit. To begin with, the initiative was with the people who called on Ezra to bring out the Book of the Law. The same sense of eagerness and expectancy is expressed in verse 3, as 'all the people listened attentively'; then in verse 5 as the people stood up when the Book was opened, and in verse 13 when 'everyone gathered to give attention to the words of the Law'.

It reminds us that there is little to be gained from reading the Bible without such expectancy. Jesus' own ministry was frustrated when there was no expectancy on the part of his hearers – he began to teach in the synagogue and was met with cynicism and incredulity. Expectant faith is the soil in which God's Word will bear fruit, and that is a lesson that is valid throughout our Christian life.

A further sign of their spiritual hunger was their seriousness. They were ready to cope with all kinds of inconvenience in order to hear this Word. The Water Gate congregation stood from daybreak to noon – for at least five hours, without a coffee break in sight – because they longed to hear and understand what God had to say to them. 'Ezra praised the LORD, the great God; and all the people lifted their hands and responded, "Amen! Amen!" Then they bowed down and worshipped the LORD with their faces to the ground' (Nehemiah 8:6).

Maybe there is something to learn from the response of the people in Jerusalem that day: a longing for God to speak as they lifted up their hands, and an attitude of reverence as they bowed with their faces to the ground (v. 6). Perhaps these too are prerequisites for understanding God's Word and coming into his presence. Indeed, the verse is important in reminding us that we don't venerate the book as such: its purpose is to bring us into the presence of its author, the Lord, the great God. Luther used to describe Scripture as the cradle in which we will find the baby. Its purpose is to draw attention not to itself, but to the person of Jesus.

At Keswick this has often meant that, alongside the preaching of Scripture, there has frequently been a call to prayer, or the supportive ministry of counselling by speakers and leaders. Very often people have attended the event in church groups, and have spent time discussing, praying and applying the Scriptures as they have climbed the Lakeland fells or had meals together. Many speakers have seen their responsibility as extending to such personal ministry. A good example is George Duncan, whose most famous ministries were at St Thomas's Church in Edinburgh and St George's Tron in Glasgow. In 1947 he spoke at the Convention for the first time. In addition to his compelling preaching, Duncan gave himself to personal spiritual counsel, spending time with those who responded to addresses. So concerned was he that God's Word should be applied personally that, in the 1960s, when Keswick was attracting thousands of newcomers, Duncan warned them against coming to the Convention expecting 'a glorified spiritual picnic'.[6] Hearing God's Word is meant to lead to change. Which brings us to final theme from the Jerusalem Convention . . .

The implications of God's grace

The Bible is not given just to inform or to instruct, but to provoke change. We should expect this, because God's Word does its work – Scripture not only says things, it does things. Tim Chester has written an inspiring book for Keswick on the theme of mission, and tells the story of someone who heard the morning Bible readings on the book of Amos, given by Alec Motyer, who, from the 1970s, gave Keswick Bible Readings over the course of four decades: 'I'm sure that during those readings . . . the Spirit was planting his seeds in the receptive soil of our souls as we struggled with whether the Lord wanted us to serve together', John told Tim. And by the end of the week John and his girlfriend were engaged to be married and went forward at the missions evening as a sign of their commitment to serve as a couple, eventually going to India.[7] God's Word does its work. And the Nehemiah story describes the response among God's people at the Jerusalem Convention.

> *The Bible is not given just to inform or to instruct, but to provoke change. God's Word does its work – Scripture not only says things, it does things.*

Dynamic impact

First, they realized that their lives had failed to match up to the standards that God had set: 'For all the people had been weeping as they listened to the words of the Law' (Nehemiah 8:9). But Ezra and Nehemiah moved quickly to set that failure within the wider context of God's purposes for his people: 'This day is holy to the LORD your God. Do not mourn or weep . . . Go and enjoy choice food and sweet drinks, and send some to those who have nothing prepared. This day is holy to our Lord. Do not grieve, for the joy of the LORD is your strength' (8:9, 10). They were to accept joyfully all that God had done for them. It was a special day, a day to recall God's grace upon them as his own people. With the encouragement of the leaders, the people went to celebrate, to eat and drink *'with great joy'*. After hours of standing, they must have headed off for the party with added enthusiasm. Now that they were finally back in Jerusalem, they had come to realize that it was God's desire to bless them: 'They now understood the words that had been made known to them' (8:12).

But there is another response to God's Word. Their new understanding of God led them to confession, and the people gathered, fasting and wearing sackcloth and putting dust on their heads (9:1). A national day of repentance and recommitment was held and the confession, like the celebration, was also provoked by reading God's Word. Anyone who has experienced the restoring grace of God in their life will want to commit themselves to living a life worthy of that calling. And so the prayer moves towards covenant renewal. It was an expression of their commitment to obeying God's Word: they were 'binding themselves with a curse and an oath to follow the law of God given through Moses the servant of God and to obey carefully all the commands, regulations, and decrees of the LORD our Lord' (10:29).

The ripple effect

That's the significance of the Jerusalem Convention: hearing God's Word, celebrating God's goodness, knowing God's grace and then obeying God's laws. It is truth in action. And that has been the driving force behind the Keswick movement. Despite their differing denominations, their diverse views on secondary issues, and their various styles and personalities, a key strength among Keswick speakers has been their serious engagement with the Scriptures, and their desire for that engagement to have a powerful impact on people's lives. The strapline for today's Keswick follows the same sequence that we find in the Jerusalem Convention, now expressed in New

Testament terms: it is *Hearing God's Word – Becoming like God's Son – Serving God's mission.*

Authentic Christians not only speak the message; their lives embody the message. That's the purpose of coming to the Bible, and the purpose of the Keswick movement. Hearing God's Word is to lead to determined faithfulness, to changed lives, to consistent Christian living. As Michael Wilcock once said: 'Our understanding of God's Word has to do with our obedience, not our brains.'

3

Proclaiming God's gospel

Every Christian should take the Bible seriously. It is the Word of God, authoritative and powerful. But one of the accusations made against those who are committed to the Bible as the Word of God is that they believe in a distorted Trinity of Father, Son and Holy Bible. They are sometimes charged with being 'bibliolaters'. But such critics misunderstand why evangelicals (who are both Bible people and gospel people) pay such careful attention to the Scriptures as the Word of God. Alister McGrath explains: 'Christianity is Christ-centred, not book-centred; if it appears to be book-centred, it is because it is through the words of Scripture that the believer encounters and feeds upon Jesus Christ. Scripture is a means not an end, a channel, rather than what is channelled.'[1]

We've seen how, on the road to Emmaus, Jesus chose not to reveal himself directly to the disciples, but deliberately placed the Scriptures before them, explaining that these pages spoke of him (Luke 24:25–27, 44–49). Of course, we more easily grasp the fact that the New Testament speaks of Jesus Christ – we understand immediately that its writers focus on

Christ, for the Scriptures 'are able to make you wise for salvation through faith in Christ Jesus' (2 Timothy 3:14–15). But, on the road to Emmaus, Jesus was pointing them back to the Old Testament Scriptures. They too spoke of him. So the whole Bible is given to us for precisely this reason – to bring us into a living relationship with Jesus Christ, the Living Word. The Bible is the Father's testimony to the Son, and we know that he is the focal point of all of Scripture. Jesus frequently made this clear. For example:

> You study the Scriptures diligently because you think that in them you have eternal life. These are the very Scriptures that testify about me.
> (John 5:39)

> If you believed Moses, you would believe me, for he wrote about me.
> (John 5:46)

> . . . the scroll of the prophet Isaiah was handed to him. Unrolling it, he found the place where it is written: 'The Spirit of the Lord is on me, because he has anointed me to proclaim good news to the poor. He has sent me to proclaim freedom for the prisoners and recovery of sight for the blind, to set the oppressed free, to proclaim the year of the Lord's favour.' Then he rolled up the scroll, gave it back to the attendant and sat down. The eyes of everyone in the synagogue were fastened on him. He began by saying to them, 'Today this scripture is fulfilled in your hearing.'
> (Luke 4:17–21)

> And beginning with Moses and all the Prophets, he explained to them what was said in all the Scriptures concerning himself.
> (Luke 24:27)

This means that we study and preach the Scriptures with the purpose of knowing Jesus and making him known.

The Keswick movement has long been known for proclaiming the good news of Jesus Christ. Early in its development, the international evangelist D. L. Moody encouraged the Keswick leaders in this area.[2] It is not that the work is especially evangelistic, although it continues to maintain an evangelistic edge around the world, urging repentance and faith in Christ. In the last few years a greater emphasis has been placed on ensuring that all events are accessible to family and friends who are not yet believers, and many have come to faith in Christ as a result. But proclaiming God's gospel is inevitable – wonderfully! – because Keswick's teaching on Christ-centred living and the call to holiness has necessarily involved a clear and comprehensive statement of the Christian gospel.

The work of the Trinity

Although Christ is at the centre, as we shall see, at the same time Keswick teaching and its consequent spirituality has been thoroughly trinitarian. We began by stressing the urgent need to know God. In the next chapter we will underline God's purpose of making us more like his Son, living under his Lordship and proclaiming his Word. And in chapter 5 we will also address the theme of the Spirit's presence and power. Keswick spirituality is trinitarian spirituality, founded firmly on the gospel of God.

At various times and in various countries, the Keswick movement has sometimes deliberately taught a sequence of gospel themes as it has addressed its core concern of spiritual renewal. This has nearly always been a helpful overview of the essence of the gospel. In the 1950s, a two-page set of instructions sent to each speaker gave an outline of the sequence of emphasis, 'to which speakers are invited to adhere as they wait upon the Lord for His particular message'. This might strike us as somewhat prescriptive, but it may well have been wise programme planning. Here's a typical sequence from that period, from Sunday evening to the following Friday:

- 'The high and lofty one whose name is holy', and the glorious inheritance of the children of God;
- Sin in the life of each person and its disastrous consequences;
- The perfect cleansing available in the precious blood of Christ;
- The wholehearted surrender of the cleansed life to God;
- The fullness of the Holy Spirit and the indwelling and abiding presence of Christ in the heart of the believer;
- The life of sacrificial service and mission which must ensue, and the means of grace to make possible a holy walk.

Not everyone liked the thematic sequence, some suggesting that to leave the Spirit's work until Thursday was hardly biblical. It was sometimes felt to be a rigid formula designed to bring Christians to a particular 'crisis moment' at which they could receive God's blessing – a special sequence of spiritual experiences to help you become holy. It led some to feel it could be rather manipulative. But it was never pushed rigidly, and speakers who had a different perspective on the pathway to holiness were still able to teach from Scripture with integrity on the theme for that day. But one great value of the outline was to ensure some steady unfolding of gospel themes. In 1959 Stephen Olford likened the development of teaching at Keswick to the unfolding of the book of Romans – he was to suggest that every minister should read Romans at least once a week right through, learning it by memory!³ Certainly there were differing perspectives on how sections of Romans were to be understood in terms of the Christian's battle with sin and the nature of new life in Christ. But the sequence represented a progression of practical doctrinal teaching, which enabled listeners to engage with the trinitarian undergirding of the call to holiness. That has always been the aim. The gospel must be at the centre.

Let's take another quick look at Ephesians 1, and an astounding sentence found in verses 3 to 14. When Paul wrote this in Greek it was in fact one long sentence – 202 words in total, without a comma or a full stop. It's an amazing, breath-taking sentence, the theme of which is the theme of the whole letter. In many senses this short passage sums up Keswick's focus too – God's plan and purpose for salvation in all its dimensions.

The Father's plan

Stephen Hawking, the mathematician and cosmologist, recently divulged that one of the most common enquiries in his mail bag is the question: 'Can you prove that God does not exist?' To which he replied: 'We are such insignificant creatures on a minor planet of a very average star in the outer suburbs of one of a hundred thousand million galaxies. So it is difficult to believe in a God that would care about us, or even notice our existence.'

Paul says exactly the opposite. 'Praise be to the God and Father of our Lord Jesus Christ, who has blessed us in the heavenly realms with every spiritual blessing in Christ . . .' (v. 3); 'He chose us in him before the creation of the world' (v. 4); 'He predestined us for adoption to sonship' (v. 5); He 'lavished' his grace on us (v. 8); and 'he made known to us the mystery of his will' (v. 9). The verbs demonstrate that it is his loving initiative – 'in accordance with his pleasure and will' (v. 5); 'according to his good pleasure' (v. 9); 'according to the plan of him who works out everything in conformity with the purpose of his will' (v. 11). And not only that. This song of praise spans past, present and future. God is in control of the whole thing! It's from one eternity past to another in the future. Everything is within the will and plan of God the Father. And that's the perspective we need in a world that seems out of control, or when our own lives seem confused or uncertain. This is quite different from Stephen Hawking's cynicism. You and I are firmly in God's will and purpose. There is nothing outside God's plan. Everything is under his control and care.

And Paul insists that God chose us in Christ (vv. 4, 5). 'Being chosen' would have registered with some of Paul's readers. The Jews were the people who always saw themselves as 'the elect'. They had been chosen. They were God's people. But now Paul is writing to everyone – to Jew and Gentile alike, to you and me too. And he makes the radical claim that all of those in Christ are chosen – and chosen even before the world began. That was clear from the beginning, of course. When God spoke to Abraham thousands of years earlier, his choice of Israel had nothing to do with elitism. God chose Abraham and his family in order, through them, to bless all the families of the earth.

He makes the point in the next chapter that Gentiles were previously outsiders, excluded, foreigners to the covenants of promise, far away from the privileges of God's people. But God's eternal plan is that they too – we too – should belong to the family. He has chosen outsiders like us to be his children: 'In love he predestined us for adoption to sonship through Jesus Christ' (v. 5). As John says, we are called God's children because that in fact is what we are! Election and adoption simply mean that we are brought into the same kind of relationship that Jesus, God's Son, enjoys.

And, more than this, we are chosen to be changed. 'He chose us in him before the creation of the world to be holy and blameless in his sight' (v. 4). 'In him we were also chosen . . . in order that we . . . might be for the praise of his glory' (vv. 11, 12).

God's purpose is to restore the image, to bring us back to his intention – a holy people, for the praise of his glory. His fatherly concern is to take our broken lives, and to make us new, make us whole, restore his good purposes in us. And through what Christ has done, and through the Spirit's indwelling presence, this is happening. Little by little, his purpose is being worked out, until that day when it will finally be brought to completion. That's the Father's plan.

Centred on Christ

Not long ago I read about a producer on the TV soap opera *Coronation Street*, who was filming a wedding scene on location in a lovely fourteenth-century church. He had removed a cross from the camera frame, hiding it behind some flowers. The report was headed: 'Nice church; shame about the cross.' As in the first century, Jesus and his cross are an embarrassment in our world. There's no doubt that it is getting more difficult these days for us to maintain our commitment to declaring Jesus Christ as the unique and only Saviour of the world. In the context of today's pluralism it's not uncommon for Christians to be asked why they are so arrogant as to claim that Jesus is for every culture.

But Paul's sentence shows us that Jesus Christ is not to be reduced to one option among many. Christianity is inescapably exclusive because of the inescapably exclusive claims about Jesus. In fact, it is not going too far to say that 'Christianity is Christ'. The God whom we worship is defined in verse 3 as 'the God and Father of our Lord Jesus Christ', and God's plan of salvation is centred on Him. If you scan the first fourteen verses and count how many references there are to Jesus Christ by name or title, there are fifteen in all.

> *Christianity is inescapably exclusive because of the inescapably exclusive claims about Jesus. In fact, it is not going too far to say that 'Christianity is Christ'.*

United with Christ

How do you define a Christian? At its most basic, a Christian is someone who is united with Christ. We are incorporated into his life. To be 'in Christ' is to be united with him, as a limb with the body or a branch with a tree. It is a living, integral, organic, vital relationship with Christ. So that's why every blessing of the new creation – every spiritual blessing (v. 3) – is ours, if we are in Christ. And it's for this reason that we are called to be holy and blameless (v. 4). How can that possibly be true? The reason is that we are 'in Christ Jesus'. The idea is repeated in verse 4. We are chosen *in him*. Before we existed, as John Stott puts it, 'God put us and Christ together in his mind'; we are adopted through Jesus Christ (v. 5) and we receive God's grace because we belong to his dearly loved Son (v. 6). So now, for the Christian, every spiritual blessing is ours because we are in Christ, united to him. And, for all Christians, whether it's facing low-level daily discouragement in our workplace or whether it's life-threatening opposition, or whether it's serious illness: whatever our circumstances, this really matters. I am now 'in Christ'. I am united to Christ, I am rooted in Christ, my life is hid in Christ.

Redeemed by Christ

This is the central point of God's plan: 'In him we have redemption through his blood' (v. 7). 'Redemption' is one of the word pictures for atonement. The root meaning is 'to set free by the payment of a price'. We are set free from the imprisonment of sin, of Satan, and from the powers of darkness and the fear of death. And the ransom price? 'Redemption through his blood.'

We know it well enough, don't we? We are slaves to sin, and, despite our determined resolve, we cannot break free. Religious people try, of course. They do all they can to win God's approval. But Ephesians 1 underlines that salvation comes only through one way, one person, one act of obedience on the cross. The Christian faith stands out from religious attitudes in a wonderfully unique way. For the message of the Christian gospel is not *what I do* but *what is done*. It is all God's work: because we were chosen before the creation of the world, before we could contribute anything; because it was Jesus who shed his blood to pay the price, and to secure our forgiveness; and that's why verse 7 declares: 'in accordance with the riches of God's grace'. Grace runs through the song, of course. His grace is far stronger than the chains of sin and death.

The breadth and depth of Christ's redeeming work have been a constant refrain in the Keswick movement, and they must never be neglected. A wonderful treatment of this theme, quoting many Keswick speakers, has been provided by Jeremy and Elizabeth McQuoid, in their passionate and moving book *The Amazing Cross*, deliberately published in the Keswick Foundation series to highlight the significance of this topic.[3]

Going back to Ephesians 1, look where the passage is heading: 'his will . . . to be put into effect when the times reach their fulfilment – to bring unity to all things in heaven and on earth under Christ' (v. 10). This describes God's ultimate purpose: on that final day, everything will be summed up to find its unity and completion in Jesus Christ the Lord.

Guaranteed by the Spirit

At the end of many meetings, Christians pray that they will all know: 'The grace of our Lord Jesus Christ, the love of God, and the fellowship of the Holy Spirit' (2 Corinthians 14:13). This, of course, reflects how the loving God and the gracious Lord Jesus are now present with us – in the person of the Holy Spirit, through whom we are to be in constant empowering fellowship with God himself. In Ephesians 1, the sentence begins in verse 3 with the hint that all God's blessings are part of the new covenant gift of the Spirit. But Paul gives us two images that describe the Spirit's ministry.

First, he describes *the seal*: 'When you believed, you were marked in him with a seal, the promised Holy Spirit' (v. 13). A seal is a mark of ownership – it's like the stamp or the brand on livestock, such as we might see on the sheep on the Cumbrian fells. But, for believers, such a brand or seal is not outward but inward – the presence of the Holy Spirit. As Paul reminded the Romans: 'If anyone does not have the Spirit of Christ, they do not belong to Christ . . . Those who are led by the Spirit of God are the children of God' (Romans 8:9–14).

And, second, the Spirit is a *deposit* to guarantee 'our inheritance until the redemption of those who are God's possession – to the praise of his glory' (v. 14). This is a well-known image from trading: if you are moving to a new flat in an expensive city such as London you have to put down a huge deposit, guaranteeing the rental agreement. As Paul told the Corinthians, God has given us the Spirit, *guaranteeing what is to come* (2 Corinthians 5:5). The Holy Spirit in our lives is the first instalment of all that will follow in eternity. His presence is God's assurance to us of a sure and certain future. And he is fully engaged in the saving work of God. Here and now, he empowers us to live our new life. He makes Jesus real to us, despite the distractions of our sinful nature and the world around us. He enables us to experience something of that future inheritance here and now, even if we are only walking in the shallows of that vast ocean we will one day experience.

Well, there we have it: the Father's plan, centred on Christ, guaranteed by the Spirit. The Keswick movement seeks to proclaim God's gospel in these varied and rich dimensions. We long to know God better – Father, Son and Holy Spirit. And this calls for a response of humility, since the great force of this passage is that every aspect of our salvation, from beginning to end, is God's doing, not ours. Christianity is not what I do, but what is done. All I have to boast about is Jesus Christ. 'By the grace of God I am what I am' (1 Corinthians 15:10).

If this trinitarian sentence in Ephesians 1 sinks into our hearts and minds, then whatever fears we face, whatever uncertainties we have regarding our life and future, we can be totally secure. We are God's dearly loved children, chosen by him before the world began, adopted into his family according to his eternal will and good purpose. We are inextricably united with Jesus Christ. We are indwelt by God himself, who marks us out as belonging to the new heavens and new earth. Our lives are totally secure, now and in eternity.

A sense of responsibility follows: we have been chosen to change. He chose us to be holy and blameless in his sight. So the strong emphasis on God's initiative is not to be taken as an excuse for passivity. Instead, it is a call to determined action – as Paul was to write later in Ephesians 4:1: 'I urge you to live a life worthy of the calling you have received.' If we are adopted into the family, we must accept the responsibility to imitate our Father and to cultivate the family likeness. We will want to be committed to living like Christ – the great theme to which we now turn.

4

Becoming like God's Son

I remember the evening vividly: a frail old man, walking stick in hand and supported by a friend, slowly climbed the steps to the Keswick platform and moved on towards the lectern. By this stage of his life he had spoken on every continent of the world, to multiple thousands in baseball stadia, to hundreds in church buildings of every denomination, to congregations gathered under trees and at many student missions, as well as to many small groups. He had been named one of *Time* magazine's 'One hundred most influential people' in 2005, awarded the CBE in the Queen's New Year's honours list the following year, and was considered one of the foremost global leaders of evangelicalism in the twentieth century. He had written over fifty books and preached thousands of sermons. As he stood to give the final address of his long career as a preacher and teacher, this is what John Stott said to a congregation of Convention delegates at Keswick in 2009:

> I want to share with you where my mind has come to rest as I
> approach the end of my pilgrimage on earth and it is – God

wants his people to become like Christ. Christlikeness is the will of God for the people of God.[1]

In addressing this most significant purpose of God for every Christian, John Stott was returning to a theme that has been part of the DNA of the worldwide Keswick movement since its earliest days. And it remains a core theme, which needs to be proclaimed and modelled today. Stott opened with three basic texts to demonstrate the biblical basis of the call to Christlikeness.

First, God has predestined his people to be conformed to the image of his Son: that is, to become like Jesus: 'For those God foreknew he also predestined to be conformed to the image of his Son, that he might be the firstborn among many brothers and sisters' (Romans 8:29). The mission of the Lord Jesus, conceived in an eternity past, was nothing other than to restore the image, to overturn the disastrous effects of the fall and to restore within us the original divine image.

Second, God has provided the Holy Spirit, by whom we are being transformed into the image of Jesus himself: 'And we all, who with unveiled faces contemplate the Lord's glory, are being transformed into his image with ever-increasing glory, which comes from the Lord, who is the Spirit' (2 Corinthians 3:18).

Third, whilst many aspects of our future home in heaven are not clear, one thing is certain: we will be like Christ: 'Dear friends, now we are children of God, and what we will be has not yet been made known. But we know that when Christ appears, we shall be like him, for we shall see him as he is' (1 John 3:2). We will be with him and like him for all eternity.

So, from the perspective of past, present and future, Scripture teaches us that this is God's purpose for every believer. We have been predestined for this in God's plans, we have been equipped for this by God's Spirit, and we will be like Christ on that final day. Nothing in life is more important. But, as Jim Packer has often noted, holiness is a neglected priority of the modern church. Although Packer has in the past been a critic of aspects of Keswick teaching, the movement fully shares his commitment to holiness and his concern about a loss among evangelicals of that emphasis. As he has expressed it: 'I put it to you that holiness is a fading glory in the evangelical world.'[2]

It's for this reason that today the Keswick movement wants once again to bring this theme to the centre of the stage. This is God's loving and sovereign purpose. But we must add that, in an age when people long for authenticity, there is no doubt that, for many non-Christians, the credibility of Christian witness often rests upon the integrity of the Christian believer. The watching world needs both to hear the gospel and to see that gospel embodied in the lives of Jesus' followers.

> *The watching world needs both to hear the gospel and to see that gospel embodied in the lives of Jesus' followers.*

The heartbeat

A concern for holiness has been the sustained heartbeat of the Keswick movement. It is a shame that today people caricature the present Keswick movement as being locked into a particular view of holiness (sometimes called 'the Keswick view'), when for the past forty years the position taken on Keswick platforms has been entirely mainstream evangelical teaching, with which few believers could disagree. And when, in the past, there might have been differing views about how holiness can be achieved, there was far more nuancing in the teaching than some critics have allowed for. Why did this happen? Here's a very quick sketch of the issues.

The quest for holiness was one that was engaging the attention of many Christians in the period when Keswick began. We've already introduced Thomas Harford-Battersby, the vicar in Keswick who was a founding father of the movement, and he was a typical example. While studying at Oxford he was initially impressed by the influential high-church Oxford Movement because, in his view, they 'introduced a far higher standard of holy living' into the Church of England.[3] But in his first curacy, in a poorer district of Portsmouth, he found that neither high-church spirituality nor the more liberal theology that he also began to explore helped him to make 'that advance in holiness which I desire'. In the 1850s he returned to his early evangelicalism but, as we saw in chapter 1, his spiritual quest continued. He longed for greater Christlikeness.

There were various vigorous debates about holiness at the time when Keswick started. Some Christians seemed to get worryingly close to the idea of sinless perfection, and others seemed to suggest that a crisis moment could secure a condition of Christlikeness, which almost implied that no personal struggle or effort was needed. (Both of these ideas have been rejected by the Keswick movement, of course, but you still hear criticism, even in respectable journals, suggesting that this remains the Keswick position. May we reaffirm: it does not!) In fact, in the early decades of Keswick it was Evan Hopkins who did most to formulate the Convention's approach to the holy life, and he was keen to show that the Convention was not portraying 'the holiness of the Christian as consisting in the eradication of sin from his own heart and life'.[4] For Hopkins, the secret of power – both to live a holy life and to be effective in Christian service – was what was called at the time 'resting faith'. By this he did not mean passivity, but active trust in Christ's work and in the empowering presence of the Spirit.

Although Keswick's particular outlook on how the Christian lives in a Christlike way – what was sometimes termed the doctrine of 'sanctification by faith' – stood in contrast to some other views of progress in the Christian life, there was also a great deal of common ground. Hopkins was at pains to show that, although there were calls at Keswick for a response of consecration, there was always room for further progress in sanctification.[5] This did not mean a return to an emphasis on human effort. The call to consecration, in the early Keswick movement, stressed that holiness was, rather, a gift to be received. Hopkins stated pithily that, by contrast with the teaching in other religious systems, which 'begin by demanding', Christ begins 'by bestowing'.

It's true that Hopkins believed that there should be a definite turning point in an individual Christian's experience. Speaking in the early twentieth century, Hopkins continued to argue for 'a definite decision for holiness, a thorough and wholehearted dedication to God'. But this, for Hopkins, was to be followed by a process – sanctification. 'Before you can draw a line', he sometimes said, 'you must begin with a point. The line is the process, the point is the crisis.' Although Hopkins was a shaper of Keswick spirituality, others wanted to affirm that his approach was one that had a solid foundation. Keswick leaders were always anxious to show that their teaching was drawn directly from Scripture and was also in tune with the sound evangelical thinking of the past.

The Lordship of Christ

In the period after the First World War, Graham Scroggie, a Baptist minister, became the foremost speaker at Keswick arguing for a new presentation of a Christ-centred approach to holiness, which he saw as mainstream evangelical orthodoxy.[6] He was particularly unhappy that, among some evangelicals, there seemed to be more emphasis on the Spirit's work in sanctification than on the work of Christ. For him, the proper emphasis was on the indwelling of Christ in the Christian, with particular emphasis on his Lordship as indispensable to Christian living and service.

Scroggie was totally committed to the exposition of the Bible, and thinking biblically about the experience of holiness was rightly a personal crusade. He wished to move away from the notion of climactic spiritual crises being essential, and also warned against anyone going back from Keswick to his or her local church to parade a superior spirituality. Here's another problem: if people have imagined that there are two categories of Christian – one of which has somehow 'arrived' or somehow been blessed by God as a spiritual elite – they have been misled. All believers stand equally at the foot of the cross, in need of God's continual grace.

Yet on a number of occasions Scroggie spoke of a decisive moment in his own life, thirteen years after his conversion, in which the Bible and Christ came alive for him in a new way. In 1942 Scroggie told the Convention audience: 'I shall never forget days of despair in my first ministry in East London.' He even told his wife he would pull out of ministry. 'I have no message', he agonized. 'I have no power; I have no joy, and it will kill me.' But when he was out walking in nearby Epping Forest, Scroggie 'met with God' and became convinced that God was telling him to make a fresh resolve to put the Bible at the centre of his ministry. Scroggie's personal story, as well as his biblical teaching, made a deep impression on Keswick.

For the past forty years or more the emphasis has been on the call for steady life transformation and growth in Christlikeness. But there has always been room at the Convention for preaching for a decision, when individuals hear God's Word, sense the Spirit's leading, and commit themselves more wholeheartedly to living for Christ. Such moments of focused intention are not crises that somehow achieve a higher level of spiritual experience, but are often manifestations of the power of God's Word and Spirit in provoking renewed repentance and faith, and a realization of the vital importance of living more fully under the Lordship of Christ.

Living like Christ

What became increasingly significant at Keswick in the twentieth century were not only the clear biblical foundations for the life of holiness, but the practical business of living a Christlike life. The Convention had moved away from the language of the 'higher Christian life', since this was seen as elitist, but there was still a perception that Keswick holiness teaching was geared to a rather privileged, upper-middle-class segment of society. Many employed people did not have the leisure time to attend conventions but, in the inter-war years, the make-up of Keswick-goers began to change. When a chairman of that period spoke about consecration having to do with 'shops, offices, workrooms, laboratories and consulting rooms', he was speaking of a world with which many more people in his Keswick audience – especially younger people – were familiar.[7]

A changing spiritual emphasis was summed up at Keswick by a Baptist leader and missionary statesman, W. Y. Fullerton,

when he referred in 1924 to the popular Keswick hymn
'Channels only' and told his listeners that, rather than simply
being channels, which could imply passivity and inactivity,
they should be God's living agents.[8] Here's some straight
speaking from W. H. Aldis, who was Home Director of the
China Inland Mission (CIM, now the Overseas Missionary
Fellowship, OMF International) and was also the Keswick
chairman either side of the Second World War. 'We are all
sick and tired of theological phrases that do not seem to lead
us anywhere,' he said, and he cited three practical reasons
why the filling of the Holy Spirit was needed: the work of
the Spirit was to make the Christian like Christ, to bring
about victory over sin, and to enable effective witness and
service.

God's work and ours

By the post-war Keswick era, any call to surrender to Christ
was likely to include practical teaching, guidance and encouragement. We must not, Scroggie insisted, rely on God to do
what we can do ourselves. He was opposed to the idea of 'Let
go – and let God', and had said that spiritual victory over
sin came through 'fighting and striving to make true in
experience what is true for us positionally'.[9] Fred Mitchell, a
Methodist layman who followed W. H. Aldis as Keswick
chairman as well as CIM Home Director in this period, was
happy to refer to the theme of 'sanctification by faith' and
even to mystical union with Christ, but when he quoted some
famous lines from the hymn-writer Frances Ridley Havergal
– 'Holiness by faith in Jesus, Not by effort of my own' –
Mitchell went on to say that this must not be taken to imply
a way of ease. Progress in the spiritual life, for him, had
been a steady climb.

It became clear from then on that Keswick leaders taught that, alongside all that God has purposed and achieved in Christ and all that God has provided for believers by the empowering presence of the Holy Spirit, active spiritual effort was needed by all Christians who wished to be Christlike.

Living in him

The Keswick movement has been governed by clear priorities, even if at times there have been varying views on certain aspects of the work of sanctification. First, as Stott taught in his final public address at Keswick, God's purpose is that his people should become like his Son. Christlikeness is the will of God for the people of God, and this message must once again take centre stage. Second, we must continually examine the Scriptures to understand how this calling is to be worked out. As we stressed in chapter 2, the overriding concern must be to live according to the truth of God's Word. And, third, our concern must be not only for correct theology but for practical holiness, expressing day by day what Christlikeness looks like in a secular world.

The New Testament encourages all Christians to grow up into Christ, and one of the most well-known expressions of that concern is in Paul's letter to the Colossians: 'He is the one we proclaim, admonishing and teaching everyone with all wisdom, so that we may present everyone fully mature in Christ. To this end I strenuously contend with all the energy Christ so powerfully works in me' (Colossians 1:28, 29). Paul gave everything he had to bring people to maturity, and he described his hopes for all believers like this: 'So then, just as you received Christ Jesus as Lord, continue to live your lives in him . . . strengthened in the faith as you were taught, and overflowing with thankfulness' (Colossians 2:6, 7).

Having received Christ, we are to live in him. To receive Christ means receiving or taking in the truth of the gospel, just as the Colossians had received that gospel. But, more than this, we have exercised faith not just in the teaching, but in Jesus himself – we have received him. This was the beginning of our new life in Christ, the start of our Christian discipleship. That's why Paul says we have received 'Christ Jesus as Lord'. We acknowledge his right to rule every area of our life. There's a direct and compelling book on the theme of 'Discipleship' in the *Keswick Foundations* series, written by Peter Maiden, which presses home this point with great effectiveness. It's a great book that stimulates wholehearted commitment to Christ.[10]

And Paul continues: just as we received Christ Jesus as Lord, *so we live in him.* It's impossible for a disciple of Jesus to say 'I've received Christ as Lord' and then fail to live a life that is dependent on him and obedient to him. You have begun your discipleship by committing yourself to Jesus Christ as Lord; now make good that profession, and shape your life by living under his Lordship. Strengthened by God's Word and by God's Spirit, we will be fulfilling God's good purpose for us: that we should become like his Son.

5

Depending on God's Spirit

For a movement committed to hearing God's Word and becoming like God's Son, depending on God's Spirit is foundational. We know that without the Holy Spirit there would be no gospel and no Bible. So one of the strengths of the Keswick movement has been its commitment to ensuring that Christians who care about Christ should also care about the Spirit; that Christians who are committed to the truth of God's Word should also be committed to the power of God's Spirit. There are several reasons why this should be the case.

First, the Spirit inspires the Scriptures. Peter reminds us that 'no prophecy of Scripture came about by the prophet's own interpretation of things. For prophecy never had its origin in the human will, but prophets, though human, spoke from God as they were carried along by the Holy Spirit' (2 Peter 1:20, 21). The biblical writers were moved by the Spirit, 'carried along' just as the wind carries along a sailing ship. The Spirit of God, working through the diverse personalities, contexts and cultures of its human authors, supervised the Scriptures that we now seek to understand, obey and proclaim.

Second, the Spirit illuminates or enlightens the hearers of Scripture. The Spirit is at work in the hearts and minds of believers, helping us to embrace that Word. Without the work of God's Spirit we could never understand the truth of the gospel. Paul makes it clear in his first letter to the Corinthians, having described how the apostles themselves received the Spirit and spoke in words taught by the Spirit: 'The person without the Spirit does not accept the things that come from the Spirit of God but considers them foolishness, and cannot understand them because they are discerned only through the Spirit . . . But we have the mind of Christ' (1 Corinthians 2:14–16).

Third, the Spirit equips believers, and this includes every believer, called to proclaim the gospel message and confess Christ's Lordship. This is impossible without the Spirit (1 Corinthians 12:3). The gifts given to the church, including to those who minister the Word, are given by the Spirit just as he determines (1 Corinthians 12:11). Our abilities both to understand and to teach the Scriptures are the work of the Holy Spirit, given to believers and to the local church.

But, more than this, we know that the Spirit is the one who first convicts us of sin and of our need of Christ, opening our hearts and minds to the truth of the gospel. As we saw from chapter 3, the Spirit brings us new life through that word of the gospel; the Spirit dwells within us, making God's love real to us and pointing us to Christ. And from Keswick's beginnings there was also a considerable stress at each Convention on the role of the Holy Spirit as the one enabling the Christian to lead a holy life.

The Spirit's empowering

Early on, some speakers used the term 'baptism of the Spirit' in describing a further experience of blessing. This inevitably provoked some debates! Most Convention leaders, probably led by H. W. Webb-Peploe, came to favour terminology that spoke about Christians seeking the 'filling of the Spirit' rather than 'Spirit baptism'.[1] But there was flexibility. In 1895 Andrew Murray, a minister of the Dutch Reformed Church in South Africa, made a huge impact when he spoke at Keswick on the baptism and filling of the Spirit. Murray had known a powerful movement of the Spirit in his own congregation in 1860 and had written at that time his devotional classic *Abide in Christ*. But, as he explained at Keswick, 'I became much exercised about the baptism of the Holy Spirit, and I gave myself to God as perfectly as I could to receive this baptism of the Spirit'. Then in 1882 he attended Keswick and realized during the words of a chorus – 'wonderful cleansing, wonderful filling, wonderful keeping' – that there was new power for him to receive.[2] He realized that the empowering of the Spirit was ongoing.

It was F. B. Meyer who did most to take the message of the empowering of the Spirit to different parts of the world. Like Murray, his own spiritual experience helped to shape Meyer's message. Meyer recalled vividly his first experience as a Keswick speaker, in 1887. During a late-night Convention prayer meeting he realized he felt too weary from overwork to think, to pray or to feel intensely. He 'shot out under the curtain' of the Keswick tent and went out of the town up the hill. The stars and the lake were both shining and, as he climbed the hill, he sensed that he received the Spirit like the breath of the wind. He said to himself: 'As I breathe in the air, so my spirit breathes in the fullness (to my capacity) of the Holy Spirit.'[3] By the 1890s Meyer was taking this message of the fullness of the Holy Spirit to audiences in North America, Europe and elsewhere. In 1903 Meyer was able to speak of the 'marvellous effect' of Keswick teaching on the continent of

Europe.[4] By 1907 the numbers attending Keswick each year for the Convention had grown to five to six thousand. As mentioned in chapter 3, at many Keswick meetings in Britain and elsewhere, the week began with teaching on sin and continued with cleansing from all sin, followed by teaching on the Lordship of Christ, and then on the Spirit-filled life. Although that sequence might at times have seemed formulaic, the intention was to ensure a proper focus on the ministry of the Holy Spirit among God's people.

The rise of Pentecostalism in the early twentieth century brought some challenges to Keswick. Graham Scroggie, whose influence at Keswick we have noted, was critical of the Pentecostal view that speaking in tongues was the necessary initial sign of Spirit baptism. He did accept that the gift of tongues might still be available to Christians, but he reacted against Pentecostal claims. In 1912, when minister of Bethesda Free Church, Sunderland, Scroggie wrote three articles for his own church magazine on the baptism of the Spirit and speaking with tongues. In these articles he argued vigorously that the spread of the idea that Christians should seek the baptism of the Spirit and with that the sign of tongues was 'bringing large numbers into bondage and error'.[5] Sunderland was then an important centre for early Pentecostalism, with Alexander and Mary Boddy hosting Pentecostal conventions in their church, All Saints, Monkwearmouth. Alexander Boddy, an evangelical vicar, tried to spread Pentecostal teaching at Keswick, but the Convention saw the Spirit's work in broader terms.

Revival

In the early twentieth century Keswick found itself closely linked with the Welsh Revival of 1904–5. In 1903 the first Llandrindod Wells Convention was held, after Jessie Penn-Lewis approached Charles Inwood, F. B. Meyer and Hopkins about the possibility of a convention in Wales. When there was an opportunity at the final meeting at Llandrindod Wells for expressions of surrender and dedication it seemed, according to *The Life of Faith* (a Keswick-related paper), as if everyone wanted to receive 'the fullness of blessing'.[6] By 1905 it was clear that a young miner, Evan Roberts, had become the principal figure in the Welsh Revival. Several Keswick leaders were determined to gain first-hand experience of what was going on, and travelled to Wales that year to hear and meet Roberts. At one meeting, when Roberts was praying with considerable fervour, F. B. Meyer was startled to hear the man sitting next to him threaten to start a hymn to 'drown it'. Meyer blurted out: 'Drown it, man, I have come all the way from London to catch it'![7]

A contingent of about three hundred people from Wales came to the 1905 Keswick Convention, and meetings were arranged in which there was opportunity for extra singing and testimonies. Arthur T. Pierson, an American missionary statesman, addressed the Convention on 'the inbreathed Spirit', and many people, deeply affected by what had been said, remained in the tent afterwards. Prayer went on until three o'clock in the morning. Later in the week, there was a further dramatic event at a Convention session when Pierson was the second speaker. It was the custom that Keswick meetings, especially in the evenings, had two speakers. In this case, Pierson, before he started speaking, called on all those who wanted God to 'refine us' to stand together. Everyone in the tent stood up. Most unusually for Keswick, the second speaker (Pierson) never began his message. Instead, prayer went on for hours. Confessions of need came from all parts of the tent.[8]

Keswick as a whole, however, had very mixed feelings. There was worry about excess. One respected Keswick commentator was to say: 'The torrent from the Welsh hills meeting the sluggish stream of English propriety threatened tumult.'[9] The direct Welsh influence on the main Convention was in fact short-lived. Yet the Welsh Revival was an indication that there was a search for the experience of the power of the Holy Spirit, and the desire for revival was again particularly evident in the early 1950s. In 1951, when there was a record attendance at Keswick – some Convention meetings attracted 6,000, with 2,000 at the youth meetings – George Duncan said he had not known a Convention at which God seemed so near. A year later a Scottish minister and evangelist, Duncan Campbell, spoke at the Convention about revival he had experienced in the Scottish Hebrides, and his dramatic story had an enormous impact.

The charismatic movement

The rise of the charismatic movement raised new questions for Keswick. By the mid-1960s the subject of the Holy Spirit and his gifts was becoming a major talking point in evangelicalism, but at this point Keswick was to take a more cautious position. At the 1964 Convention, John Stott's book *Baptism and Fullness* was recommended by the Keswick Council chairman. Stott's book on the work of the Holy Spirit argued against a post-conversion experience of the baptism of the Spirit. Another Anglican speaker, Maurice Wood, similarly recommended Stott's book, as well as Graham Scroggie's approach to the baptism of the Spirit. Wood's advice to his listeners was to concentrate on teaching practical holiness. Leith Samuel, a Free Church speaker, argued that the evidence for being filled by the Spirit was not unusual temporary experiences but a continued increase in Christlikeness.

There were conciliatory voices too and, since those days, evangelicals have increasingly acknowledged the common convictions that they share across denominations and party positions. We all believe in the vital importance of a common commitment to the unique work of Christ, and to his Lordship. We all acknowledge our desperate need of the Spirit's work. We are increasingly aware of the importance of standing together as fellow evangelicals, rather than sustaining controversies. Whilst this is not true in every part of the world, by and large the debates about the Spirit are no longer dominant.

> We all acknowledge our desperate need of the Spirit's work. We are increasingly aware of the importance of standing together as fellow evangelicals, rather than sustaining controversies.

The Spirit's work

But might there be a danger that we have somehow domesticated his presence and work? Do we remain committed to seeking his presence and empowering? Let's summarize why we must once again emphasize the Spirit's work.

For a movement that sees the preaching of Scripture as foundational, we know that, whenever we come to hear God's Word taught, we will want to affirm that the Spirit is within us and among us. All of us must seek his illuminating presence as we open Scripture. And every preacher must depend upon him. 'Men might be poor and uneducated, their words might be broken and ungrammatical; but if the might of the Spirit attended them, the humblest evangelist would be more successful than the most learned divine or the most eloquent of preachers,' said the great Baptist preacher C. H. Spurgeon.[10] Paul proclaimed the Word, as he said to the Thessalonians, 'not simply with words, but also with power, with the Holy Spirit and deep conviction' (1 Thesssalonians 1:5). But in the very next verse he demonstrated that the Spirit was also at work in the listeners, in the Thessalonians themselves, enabling them to welcome that Word: 'You became imitators of us and of the Lord, for you welcomed the message in the midst of severe suffering with the joy given by the Holy Spirit' (1 Thesssalonians 1:6). So, as we gather together to hear God's Word, whether at our local church or at a convention, the Spirit will be at work to convict us of sin, to convince us of God's mercy, to confirm within us God's love, to point us to the Lord Jesus, and to equip us to live Christlike lives.

Paul prays that believers will grow in their understanding through the work of the Spirit. In the trinitarian prayer of Ephesians 1, which we looked at earlier, it's important to notice the significance of the relationship between prayer, the Holy Spirit and our understanding:

> I keep asking that the God of our Lord Jesus Christ, the glorious Father, may give you the Spirit of wisdom and revelation, so that you may know him better. I pray that the eyes of your heart may be enlightened in order that you may know the hope to which he has called you, the riches of his glorious inheritance in his holy people, and his incomparably great power for us who believe.
> (Ephesians 1:17–19)

Do we not long to know God better?
If we do, then listening to God's Word in this prayerful, reflective mode, seeking the Spirit's illuminating presence and power, is vital for every believer committed to that highest goal.

Do we not long to live for Christ?
We become like him as the Spirit produces his fruit in our

lives: *love, joy, peace, patience, kindness, goodness, faithfulness, gentleness and self-control* (Galatians 5:22–23).

Do we not long to serve God's mission?

We have already referred to Andrew Murray's address at Keswick in 1895, and Tim Chester refers to something else that Andrew Murray said on that occasion: 'If we are to be real missionaries, if we are to give our money as we ought to give, and give ourselves and our children, and pray as we ought to pray, and live as we ought to live, we must have nothing less than the power of the Holy Spirit flowing freely in us to overflowing. Oh, Keswick thou canst not do the right mission work unless the Holy Spirit fill every heart. Oh Christ, we want to love and die like Thee, for God's Kingdom! Give Thine own Spirit within us!'[11]

It's an urgent prayer for our day too.

6

Uniting God's people

A while ago I was travelling from London to Warsaw, and was waiting in departures at Heathrow Airport, that place of weeping and gnashing of teeth. I was joined at the table by a Polish man returning home to visit his elderly mother after many years away. He knew that there had been significant changes in the country and he expressed his uncertainty about going back. He explained that he was working with Japanese airlines, living in Australia, and now he was hoping for a job in Poland. Then without embarrassment he confessed: 'I have no idea who I am or where I belong.' It wasn't simply that he had Polish nationality, was living in Australia and was working in Asia. It was a much more deep-seated disorientation. And this is probably one of the most common complaints, not only in today's youth culture, but among many people of all ages. There is a deep crisis of belonging.

All kinds of factors have contributed to this disorientation and rootlessness, but one of the most significant is the fracturing of social relationships of all kinds. Few of us are spared the pain of the broken relationships that are all around us.

The sense of emotional isolation and social alienation that the psychiatrists comment on is, for many, an almost daily reality.

It's no wonder that those who wish to encourage the church in its task of mission urge us to reflect on the importance of one overarching biblical theme: the importance of true Christian community. To understand and live by the biblical teaching on the unity of God's people will today be counter-cultural. It will be deeply attractive in a world of social alienation.

When Paul wrote to the Ephesians he was especially concerned to help them understand God's new society. 'You are no longer foreigners and strangers, but fellow citizens with God's people,' he wrote (Ephesians 2:19). We belong to God. And although we have commented on the alienation of living in a world of fractured relationships, Paul highlights an even more deep-seated and radical alienation in this passage: 'Remember that at that time you were separate from Christ, excluded from the citizenship in Israel and foreigners to the covenants of promise, without hope and without God in the world' (Ephesians 2:12).

Becoming a Christian means a radical change of allegiance. We are transferred out of a community under judgment and into a new community, the people of God.

Before we came to know Jesus Christ we were separated from God, we were foreigners and strangers, without hope. But Jesus' mission was to bring us home, to reconcile us to God and to each other. 'But now in Christ Jesus you who were once far away have been brought near by the blood of Christ' (Ephesians 2:13). Becoming a Christian means a radical change of allegiance. We are transferred out of a community under judgment and into a new community, the people of God. So we are now 'fellow citizens with God's people and members of his household'. As members of God's family we have instant and intimate access to him: 'you have been brought near by the blood of Christ' (2:13). In fact, the main idea in this passage is that through Jesus we are not only brought near to God, but we are also reconciled to one another – in this case the really big issue Paul addresses is the division between Jew and Gentile, brought together as fellow citizens under God's rule. Now they are united as God's children in one family.

We know that this is a radical statement in today's world, with its increasing tribalism and division. Fracture lines are everywhere – divisions over wealth, religion, class and ethnicity. But Paul declares that, in the Christian community, 'there is no Gentile or Jew, circumcised or uncircumcised, barbarian, Scythian, slave or free, but Christ is all and is in all' (Colossians 3:11). All of the previous divisions are part of the old humanity. If we are now reconciled to God, and brought to know him as Father, then we are reconciled to one another; we are part of the family. We can't have one without the other. As Paul tells the Galatian believers, 'you are all one in Christ Jesus' (Galatians 3:28).

All one in Christ

From its beginning, Keswick was determined to be inter-denominational. The Convention motto was taken from the Galatians verse we have just quoted. 'All one in Christ Jesus' was proposed by Robert Wilson, a Quaker, and today the banner headline appears above pulpits and lecterns across the world. Anglicans predominated from the early years onwards, but more Free Church people began to attend, and by 1895 Webb-Peploe was even complaining that he and

Handley Moule might lose their influence in the Church of England if the trend continued for new Keswick speakers to be 'Dissenters'![1] But there never was any possibility of a Free-Church takeover. Estimates in the 1920s and 1930s suggested that at least 60% of those attending Keswick were Church of England.[2] Free-Church participation varied according to denomination. Baptists were the second largest group at Keswick, and members of the Brethren were significant in the inter-war period, with their Sunday-morning 'breaking of bread' held in Keswick's Pavilion building during the Convention and attracting up to 700 worshippers.[3]

It was F. B. Meyer who did most in the early decades to help Keswick to transcend denominational boundaries. This wider vision was later taken up by others, and Keswick speakers have very rarely raised specific denominational issues. Meyer did occasionally take advantage of the Keswick platform to address specific ecclesiastical groups. Clergymen, including high churchmen, were urged by Meyer to pray for their local Baptist and Salvation Army neighbours.[4] Meyer saw the teaching of the inner life as naturally leading to 'a wider view of the divine constitution of the Church of Christ'.[5] When there were controversies in the early 1920s over whether Keswick should enter a 'broader path' in its spiritual expression, Meyer and Stuart Holden, who was vicar of St Paul's, Portman Square, London, and was the Keswick chairman in the 1920s, worked hard to defuse the tension.[6] As a mark of the esteem in which Meyer was held by Anglicans and Nonconformists, he was chosen in 1928 to preside at the first Communion service held in the Keswick tent.

The difficulty of achieving and maintaining evangelical unity became evident in the later 1920s. In 1926 George Buchanan, a London vicar and Keswick supporter, stated that a number of evangelicals, many of whom 'owe everything to

Keswick', were being led to 'express Keswick in Anglican terms'. He and his colleagues began to plan their own Anglican convention at Cromer, Norfolk, and this was launched in 1928. Cromer had some years of influence within Anglicanism, but came to an end after the Second World War. W. H. Aldis, who became Keswick chairman, wisely led the Convention away from controversy.

In earlier chapters we have commented on the varying views among speakers, some of which might have challenged the movement and threatened to destroy its credibility. Yet time and again, the call has been the same: as Paul expressed it, 'Make every effort to keep the unity of the Spirit through the bond of peace' (Ephesians 4:3).

Global evangelical unity

One important aspect of Keswick's contribution to evangelical unity were the supra-national links that Keswick helped to forge among evangelicals. By the First World War 'Keswicks' were being held in scores of centres, including (in England) Norwich, Manchester, Liverpool, Newcastle, Carlisle, Nottingham, Harrogate, Exeter, Weston-super-Mare, Weymouth and the Isle of Wight. A number of these were of significant size. Wales, Scotland and Ireland also developed their own convention life. In Wales, Llandrindod Wells has had an important role. In Scotland, the north of Scotland's Strathpeffer Convention has had a continued influence, and Keswick has also been represented at a convention in Buckie, in the north-east of Scotland, as well as elsewhere. In Northern Ireland the Portstewart Convention became a significant force, reflecting the strength of evangelicalism in the province. Speakers at Keswick who represented Irish life included Charles Inwood (a Methodist), James Dunlop (a Presbyterian), and

A. W. Rainsbury (an Anglican). There were also links between Keswick and Irish evangelicals in the Dublin area. A convention serving this area was held at Greystones. So the Convention forged links between England, Scotland, Ireland and Wales.

Links were also made across the globe. In 1910 F. B. Meyer gave a report at the Convention on his travels on behalf of the movement over the previous three years. His visits had included South Africa, Bulgaria, Constantinople, Ceylon, China, Nigeria and the United States. Meyer's overall impression, from his unique international perspective, was that the Keswick movement contained the spiritual message for which the world was waiting.[7] In the decades after the Second World War it was George Duncan, whose parents had been missionaries, who was most comfortable with an international role. Duncan spoke in 1975 of the variety that existed in conventions associated with Keswick, from the massive Maramon Convention at Kerala, South India, where numbers could rise above 100,000, to much smaller conventions, such as that in Hokkaido, Japan. In one year, 1958, Duncan addressed convention gatherings in Australia and New Zealand, North America, southern Africa, Kenya and Uganda. Duncan was impressed by the variety of expressions of Keswick spirituality. Some, he said, were marked by a dignity of worship. At others there was much greater spontaneity of expression, as in Jamaica, Africa, and South America.[8]

Today, as Charles Price, another world traveller on behalf of Keswick, has noted, there are – for example – conventions in the beautiful mountainous region of Hakone in central Japan; on the cool uplands of Mount Tamborine near Brisbane, Australia; in different cities in Asia and North America; and in the Caribbean islands of Barbados, Trinidad, and the Cayman Islands.[9] In the Cayman Islands, out of a population of about 20,000, the Keswick meetings, which began in the later part of the twentieth century, attracted up to 500 people. Perhaps Australia has more 'Keswick' Conventions per head of the population than any other country, with gatherings in seven or more locations.

The doctrine of difference

Of course, there have at times been tensions over differences of emphasis, but over the 140 years of Keswick's life the movement has contributed significantly to trans-denominational and trans-national evangelical unity. But we should be careful not to be complacent. Having a motto or banner headline, *All one in Christ*, is commendable, but what really matters is expressing that unity in our churches and in our evangelical partnerships. And there is still more to be done, especially in helping churches to live by a biblical 'doctrine of difference'.

All speakers are reminded of these priorities. Here is how it is expressed: 'All who speak on behalf of Keswick Ministries are asked to display sensitivity and generosity of spirit on the wide range of issues where evangelicals, in good conscience, hold a variety of opinions. Founded on our unity in Christ and our shared understanding of evangelical truth, we expect those who minister among us to expound Scripture with clarity and faithfulness, but respectfully ask them not to use the Keswick platform to campaign for particular positions on such secondary issues. Recognizing that Scripture allows for legitimate difference on such matters (Romans 14:1 – 15:13), we lay these aside for the purposes of our ministry together.'

Inevitably, there are matters today that test this resolve. At a recent Convention the theme of *Creation, Chaos and Christ* was addressed, and there was some lobbying regarding the

exact interpretation of Genesis 1 to 3 that would be taught.
The Council prepared some notes for those who might want
to campaign for particular positions, stating:

> Our purpose is to preach the certainties of the Bible faithfully.
> Keswick deliberately avoids taking a position on issues where
> the evangelical community will have diversity of opinion.
> We hold to an evangelical statement of faith, which we see as
> stating primary truth which all evangelicals affirm, but allow
> for diversity in all secondary matters, and therefore deliberately
> do not adopt a position on such issues . . . We ask all speakers
> not to favour one position over against another, but rather to
> emphasize the core issues with which we are all in agreement,
> demonstrating their biblical foundation and helping us to
> present these issues to non-Christian friends. We unashamedly
> emphasize the big issues of biblical teaching, and restrict
> ourselves to these priorities.

The same might be said with regard to the vexed issue of the
role of women. In today's evangelicalism the matter continues
to divide fellow believers. In good conscience, and with a shared
commitment to submitting to Scripture, evangelical leaders
have come to differing positions with regard to a woman
speaking to a mixed audience. The Keswick movement has not
escaped these tensions, even though over the years it has been
a substantial force in encouraging the wider ministry of women
in the church and in the cause of mission. But the movement
has sought to encourage evangelicals to stay together, and
explained this some years ago when signalling its decision to
reintroduce women speakers at the UK Convention:

> The predominant note throughout the Convention's history
> has been one of joyful unity. Such unity is expressed by virtue

of the fact that other denominational and sectarian differences have not been allowed to dominate or distract. The diverse opinions on a range of issues – spiritual gifts, the second coming, church order, baptism, and much else – have not been allowed to threaten such unity. Instead, in line with the New Testament 'doctrine of difference', fellow Christians have enjoyed mature fellowship whilst learning to agree to differ on many of these issues.[10]

And by God's grace, this has indeed proved to be the case.

Many voices, one sound

When John looked into heaven, his vision included the heavenly choir 'from every nation, tribe, people and language' (Revelation 7:9). But, significantly, the choir is singing with one voice. There is no confusion of tongues. They are there in heaven because of Christ's work, and this universal family shouts with a voice of unanimity that 'salvation belongs to our God'. But we are not to wait until heaven before we show this kind of harmony and solidarity. As far as Jesus was concerned, this unity is essential to the effectiveness of our worldwide mission, *so that the world might believe* (John 17:23).

Have you ever tried to nod your head and say 'No' or shake your head and say 'Yes'? I once visited Bulgaria in the 1980s, and had not been told that at that time they had different cultural signals from my country. Shaking your head meant 'yes'. So, as I preached, I saw the heads shaking and I thought I should preach more passionately – and the heads shook more energetically! If we did this in my culture, we would be giving two contradictory signals at same time. And yet this is one of the main problems in Christian mission. We say 'yes', we are all one in Christ, but at the same time we shake our heads

– our disagreements, our divisions communicate a very different message.

During the Balkan wars I was able to visit Christians in Serbia, and was moved by the experience of praying with a group of Christians from both Croatia and Serbia who preceded it by standing and linking arms to sing 'Bind us together': 'There is only one God, there is only one King, there is only one body, that is why we sing, bind us together.' And we have seen that that is what Paul argued as he urged believers to live in unity. There is one God, one Lord, one Spirit, one body – he goes on to name seven unities in Ephesians 4, and then appeals to us: 'Make every effort to keep the unity of the Spirit through the bond of peace' (Ephesians 4:3).

The gospel of Christ dismantles the barriers of race, economic status, gender and ethnicity, and the Christian church truly declares that 'there is neither Jew nor Gentile, neither slave nor free, nor is there male and female, for you are all one in Christ Jesus' (Galatians 3:28). At a time when the evangelical community seems to be in danger of fracturing still further into a growing number of tribes and parties, *uniting God's people* must remain a core priority for the Keswick movement today.

7

Seeking God's face

Most of us receive newsletters from Christian agencies or missionary organizations, or perhaps from our own local church, where two words are invariably linked: they are 'Prayer and Praise'. And of course they belong together. But while there has rightly been considerable interest in developing worship in our churches – with new songwriting, wider use of instruments, development of different musical traditions, and a more integrated approach to worship services – the other partner in the couplet seems to have been neglected. Prayer. Certainly in the Western world, evangelicals know they are not doing well. And as we write about the priorities and core convictions of the Keswick movement, we have to declare the same. Today, prayer is not what it should be, and we have much to learn as we reflect on how God worked among his people, both around the world and in our recent past.

When Billy Graham spoke at Keswick in 1975, he listed several features of the Keswick movement that had been significant globally, one of which was the place of prayer in Keswick spirituality. Certainly, prayer played an important part

in the shaping of the movement from its earliest days. We have
referred to the simple but moving prayer of Harford-Battersby:
'Our prayer was for deep, clear, powerful teaching, which would
take hold of the souls of the people, and overwhelm them, and
lead them to a full, definite, and all-conquering faith in Jesus.'[1]
After one address by Charles Fox in 1884 there was 'a great deep
silence of prayer'.[2] And we have mentioned in chapter 5 that
sometimes prayer gatherings ran on well into the night, as
God's people sought his face and longed for his blessing.

Praise has also been a central element at Keswick from its
beginning, and much of the spirituality of the Convention has
been expressed not only through the preaching but through
corporate devotion in song. The Convention's first hymnbook,
Hymns of Consecration and Faith, was compiled in 1875 by
James Mountain, and it went through various revisions over
the years. The main sections in the Keswick hymnbooks
covered themes such as longing for holiness, consecration,
faith, the filling of the Spirit, the overcoming life, working
for Christ and the Second Advent. The theme song of the
Convention became the hymn beginning with the evocative
words 'Full Salvation! Full Salvation!'

Take my life

Someone who had a great influence on Keswick worship was
the hymn-writer Frances Ridley Havergal, the daughter of a
Church of England clergyman. She came into an experience of
consecration and transformation in 1873, towards the end
of her short life. 'I saw it', she said, 'as a flash of electric light.'
The best known of Havergal's hymns were 'I am trusting thee,
Lord Jesus' (1874), 'Take my life and let it be consecrated, Lord,
to thee' (1874), and 'Who is on the Lord's side?' (1877). She
wrote some fifty hymns and about two hundred poems. In

1880 *The Life of Faith* carried an article on 'Miss Havergal's experience of the Deeper Life'. The hymn 'Take my life and let it be', it suggested, 'may be said to have lifted Christians of all denominations to a higher standard of devotedness, and has preached the doctrine of the Deeper Life in a most engaging and persuasive manner.'[3] Havergal's hymn 'Like a river glorious' (1878) was seen as summing up the Convention message. Writing in 1907, F. S. Webster, then rector of All Souls, Langham Place, where John Stott was later rector, quoted what he felt were crucial lines from this hymn:

> Stayed upon Jehovah, Hearts are fully blest,
> Finding as He promised, Perfect peace and rest.[4]

Although there were many hymns that emphasized holiness, there were also some that called those at Keswick to missionary service. W. Y. Fullerton wrote one hymn that was widely used, especially in the missionary context: 'I cannot tell, how He whom angels worship'. In 1946 the comment was made about this hymn being sung at Keswick: 'You only have to hear that great congregation sing Dr Fullerton's magnificent missionary hymn to the familiar *Londonderry Air* to know what singing in the Spirit really is!' Hymns of consecration were intended to reinforce the message that was being taught. In case they became too sentimental about the subject, an earlier generation of Keswick-goers was told that holy living was more important than going around with *Hymns of Consecration and Faith* under one's arm.[5]

Worship together

A major change in worship at Keswick took place over fifty years after the Convention started, when a united service of

Holy Communion was introduced. It was Stuart Holden, whose ministry in London and at Keswick offered inspiration to many, who made a call in 1920 in *The Christian* for a united Communion service at Keswick – in line with the motto 'All one in Christ Jesus'. This, he acknowledged, might be seen as challenging the discipline of the Church of England. At that point Anglican–Free Church inter-communion was not common and was not officially sanctioned by the Church of England. Holden's view was that 'any Church that can be broken up by the plain observance of the will of God . . . ought to be broken up'. Even more controversially, he added: 'The cleavage of such a Church would mean no loss whatever to the real interests and concerns of the Kingdom of God – but positive gain.' (!)[6]

No action was taken at the time, partly because of differing perspectives (especially Anglican and Free Church), and in 1926 Henry Pickering, the editor of the Open Brethren magazine, *The Witness*, suggested that 'Bethesda' (the Brethren assembly in Keswick) was the only place in the town where worshippers met 'apart from party, sect, denomination, garb, or other man-made marks',[7] This was a challenge by the Brethren to what they saw as Keswick's acceptance of denominational labels and clerical distinctions. Two years later, the Keswick Council agreed that 'the present time was most opportune for a manifestation of love and unity, such as would be shown in a United Service of Communion'.[8]

From the time of the first Keswick Communion service, clergy and lay people took part on the same basis in leading and serving at what was a deliberately non-ritualistic service. In 1933, when the Keswick chairman W. H. Aldis (assisted by another Anglican minister, a Baptist minister and two laymen) presided at the Communion service, which was attended by 3,000 people, *The Life of Faith* commented that 'members of

the Brethren must have felt themselves in the familiar atmosphere of the breaking of the bread; the Free Churchman
might have been worshipping in his own church . . . the
Anglican, accustomed to approaching the Lord's Table, must
have been thankful that on this occasion the Holy Table
waited upon him'. Even Anglican bishops such as Bishop
Taylor Smith were not necessarily given a special place at the
Communion service. This is not to say that Communion was
taken lightly; it has often been said that Communion services
– often attended by crowds of young people at the close of
their week together – have been characterized by a joyful
solemnity. In 1959 it was estimated that 5,000 people took part
in Communion, a remarkable expression of evangelical unity.
Inter-communion was, therefore, something that was to some
extent pioneered in the context of worship at Keswick.

The power of prayer

These days, of course, vibrant worship, expressed through a
rich diversity of instruments, musicians, vocalists and congregations, is a hallmark of many Conventions. In common with
developments across the evangelical family, the Keswick
movement has sought to declare God's glory through sung
worship, and around the world there is great variety, from
choirs to bands with a funky bass, to string quartets and
unaccompanied singing. We are enriched by all of these
differences.

But what about prayer?

There's no question that a movement that seeks to take
God's Word seriously must sustain the priority of prayer too.
Indeed, this lies right at the heart of our longing to know God,
as we have stressed in chapter 1. Jim Packer expressed it
memorably in his classic book *Knowing God*, where he said:

'How can we turn our knowledge *about* God into knowledge *of* God? The rule for doing this is demanding but simple. It is that we turn each truth that we learn *about* God into a matter of meditation *before* God, leading to prayer and praise *to* God.'[9]

At the early Keswicks intensity in prayer was often palpable. In the first decades of the Convention, songs such as 'Search me, O God! My actions try' were used as prayers of contrition. Many of the people present might kneel during prayer. Prayer circles were initiated among Keswick-goers, and these were regarded as affecting the atmosphere of the Convention. They had as their motto 'I will pour out my Spirit upon all flesh'. Prayer in the Keswick context had a significant effect on the Baptist denomination in Britain. In 1887 F. B. Meyer suggested the formation of a 'prayer union' of Baptist ministers. He explained that he had met with clergymen and ministers in all parts of the country who were 'anxiously seeking more spiritual power to meet the unrest and worldliness of our times'.[10] As the Baptist Ministers' and Missionaries' Prayer Union (as it was named) developed, Meyer arranged conferences, or 'retreats', covering typical Keswick themes: 'confession and consecration' and 'power for service'. Membership was 770 by 1896, out of a total of about 2,000 Baptist ministers.

> *There's no question that a movement that seeks to take God's Word seriously must sustain the priority of prayer.*

Another strong advocate of the power of prayer in the early years of Keswick was the Methodist Charles Inwood. In 1898, in a service in a Chinese church in Tungchou, Inwood gained an impression that some of the Christians present would be martyred. He promptly told them so. His message, which not surprisingly produced a 'solemn awe', was about glorifying God through martyrdom. Inwood admitted that the scene later faded from his memory until one day he read in the paper about the massacre of Christians at Tungchou. In Peking, Inwood held large meetings for Chinese Christians in the afternoons and for missionaries in the evenings. A united Communion service was held at the end of the visit. Inwood claimed that, for the first time ever in Peking, a large group of Chinese Christians – over 1,000 – sat down at the Lord's Table and shared in Communion with missionaries. Inwood also visited the extreme west of China, travelling 1,600 miles up the Yangtse. The visionary founder of the China Inland Mission, Hudson Taylor, joined Inwood's party. In one meeting of Chinese pastors and workers, Inwood recorded, the Holy Spirit was powerfully present and prayers that followed the addresses contained broken-hearted confessions and longings for holier lives of Christian service.[11]

In 1938 a Chinese Christian leader, Watchman Nee, came to Keswick. He subsequently became very well known through his widely circulated books, such as *The Normal Christian Life*. Watchman Nee was only a visitor to Keswick, not a speaker. At that time, Japan had invaded China, and there was great suffering among the Chinese people. It was reported at Keswick that year that 60 million refugees had been rooted out of their homes with nowhere to go. A report was given at the Keswick missionary meeting about some of the sufferings taking place in the country and, following that report, the Keswick chairman, W. H. Aldis, who knew the Chinese scene well, invited Watchman Nee to lead the congregation in prayer. The annual report for that year describes his prayer as 'the crowning moment of vision. No-one who was privileged to be present can forget these moments, for the very Spirit of our Lord Himself breathed through that prayer'.

Nee acknowledged the sovereignty of God in China and Japan, then went on to say: 'We do not pray for Japan. We do not pray for China. But we pray for the interests of Thy Son in China and in Japan. We do not blame any men. They are only tools in the hand of the enemy of the Lord.' A deep impression was made through this single prayer.[12]

And the Convention has also inspired significant prayer movements, some of which continue to this day. This small book is being published to mark the 140th anniversary of the UK Keswick, and we hope that at this event we will be able to note another significant milestone: 2015 is the centenary of the Fellowship of Faith for Muslims, a movement that started at the Keswick Convention. It was in 1915 that Samuel Zwemer spoke at Keswick, and his message gave birth to the FFM prayer movement, with the first meetings taking place at the Convention. There have been annual prayer conferences over the years, and a sustained commitment to producing monthly prayer bulletins. For many years FFM was the only provider of information about the Muslim world, carrying news from a variety of mission agencies, as well as news of spiritual breakthroughs around the Muslim world.

We long that that the evident power in prayer should be sustained in the Keswick movement around the world today. Anyone who has been involved with the churches of the majority world will know that we in the Western world have much to learn from them when it comes to seeking God's face in prayer. And if the Keswick movement is to practise the priorities expressed in this book, then we must also address this foundational need to seek God's face.

8

Serving God's mission

From my home in Oxford I often drive to London on the M40. Shortly before joining the M25, the traffic gets heavy and often comes to a standstill. I sat in the traffic jam for a while the other day, and noticed a field to my left, bounded by a high fence. And on the fence a graffiti artist had written a large message to the drivers stuck in traffic. It was just seven words: *Why do I do this every day?*

That's not a bad question to ask. What are the roots of our motivation to live for Christ day by day? And why do we serve God's people and seek to fulfil God's mission? In fact, the basic motivation relates to all that we have looked at in this small book. If we hear God's Word, and if we are becoming like Christ, then we will want to serve God's mission.

Paul explained his motives when replying to his critics in Corinth, who had suggested that he was involved in Christian ministry for nothing other than personal gain. He was trying to build his own reputation; he was strengthening his personal prestige, to build a power base for his growing personal empire. His critics were questioning his motives for Christian service.

So Paul replied very directly to those accusations and in 2 Corinthians 5 he demonstrated that a wholehearted commitment to Christ lay at the heart of his motivation. We'll return to these basic motivations at the end of the chapter.

In its earliest period, Keswick was reluctant to become involved in issues of world mission. The Convention leaders felt that to have a special missionary meeting would be a distraction from the main purpose of the Convention. In what became a famous comment, an early chairman, Henry Bowker, declared that missions meant 'secretaries quarrelling for collections: it would spoil Keswick'.[1] But Eugene Stock, the far-seeing secretary of the Church Missionary Society, later reflected that it was inevitable that some of those who had come to a point of dedication at Keswick would want to offer themselves for service overseas. It was not that the Keswick fathers discouraged mission or were reluctant to see money channelled overseas. Rather, their reservations were based on worries that the Convention might be diverted from its goal and even taken over by missionary bodies intent on gaining recruits and securing funds.

Inevitable momentum

The turning point came in 1885, when a Liverpool solicitor, Reginald Radcliffe, known for using a London theatre for evangelism and for other global evangelistic efforts, invited some friends to join him at a missionary prayer meeting at the Convention. The Convention often issued cautions about unauthorized meetings, but in this case the launch of an unofficial prayer meeting not only proved to be a risk worth taking but was to bring a change of heart to Keswick. Among those who attended were Eugene Stock, Barclay Buxton (who was Webb-Peploe's curate and would go to Japan five years later with the Church Missionary Society), and Archibald Orr-Ewing, who was to serve with the China Inland Mission. Despite the fact that it was not publicly announced, the prayer meeting attracted a capacity crowd. By the end of the Convention week, it led to a small group of Cambridge under-graduates standing up in a testimony meeting and offering themselves for overseas service. From the 1880s there has been a strong link between Keswick and the missionary imperative and at times hundreds of young people have stood up at Keswick in response to the missionary appeal.

A crucial influence on the shift in Keswick's perspective on mission was Hudson Taylor, the founder of the China Inland Mission. Taylor contributed to a further missionary break-through that took place at Keswick in 1887. A Church Missionary Society missionary, Longley Hall, had written to Henry Bowker from Jerusalem to ask if he would make an appeal to the Convention for help. The request was for women ('of education and private means') to go out to Palestine under the auspices of the Church Missionary Society (CMS).[2] The ladies who were wanted in Palestine were to finance themselves, which undercut Bowker's objection to Keswick involving itself with funds. On the Saturday at the end of the 1887 Convention, the Keswick tent was used for a missionary meeting. Radcliffe chaired the event and Hudson Taylor was the first speaker. At least thirty young people spoke about overseas service over the next few days.

The missionary imperative

Although in the early twentieth century the Convention continued to state that its message was not primarily about evangelism or foreign missions, it was customary for anything between 100 and 400 young people to respond to calls for dedication to overseas mission work, at a meeting held at the end of the Convention. In 1938, a remarkable 550 young people indicated their willingness to take seriously the missionary appeal.[3] It is impossible to say how many of these went overseas, but certainly many missionary societies gained candidates from Keswick. The response continued in the period immediately after the Second World War. In 1950, for example, 200 young people stood at the appeal. It was probably the first half of the twentieth century that saw the most powerful missionary output from the Convention.

The pattern for the missionary meetings remained substantially the same for a considerable time. There was no mention of any individual society at the meetings, and sermons did not dominate. Instead, a number of people who were ready to leave for mission overseas, or those who were on home leave, were to speak briefly, often for only two or three minutes. They talked about their own experience and the way in which this related to 'the claim of Christ to His people's willing service in the cause of the Evangelisation of the world'. The variety of the testimonies meant that the three hours – later reduced to two – seemed 'the shortest of all the Keswick meetings'. On occasions the pattern of the missionary meeting might be altered. In 1913, for example, J. H. Oldham, secretary of the continuation committee of the highly significant World Missionary Conference that was held at Edinburgh in 1910, gave a review of the world mission scene. Gradually the format changed as the twentieth century progressed.

The missionary imperative involved women as well as men. The first Keswick missionary, Louisa Townsend, went out at her own expense and undertook missionary work in Palestine. Townsend was followed overseas in 1893 by Amy Wilson Carmichael, who went to Japan and later to India. Amy Carmichael, who became famous within worldwide evangelicalism through her Dohnavur Fellowship in India and through such devotional classics as *His Thoughts Said . . . His Father Said* and *If*, was the first missionary to go out with funding behind her channelled through the Keswick Mission Committee.[4] The missionary meeting in 1898 heard a memorable address from Pandita Ramabai from India, who was an outstanding scholar of Sanskrit, a Bible translator and a social reformer. She had been baptized as a Christian believer in 1883, and later set up a women's community, Mukti. At Keswick in 1898 she spoke, as she described it, for the 140 million Hindu women in India. Three years previously, she stated, she had learned via a missionary from Keswick about receiving the Holy Spirit, and apart from that experience she could never have been of spiritual use. Her vision was for 1,000 Spirit-filled women to empower other Indian women and then for 100,000 Indian Christian women to spread the gospel in that country.[5]

Mission and spirituality

In other examples, a missionary with the Church of Scotland, Marion Stevenson, who was working among the Kikuyu in Africa, recalled at Keswick in 1916 how an earlier Bridge of Allan Convention had been crucial in her experience. 'I believe', she said, 'that neither my health nor my courage would stand the strain of the life I have lived out here, were it not for the enabling and keeping power of the Holy Spirit.' In 1937 Keswick was challenged by a fresh spiritual movement when a missionary in Ruanda (now Rwanda), Stanley Smith, related how open confession of sins, which had begun among Africans, had subsequently spread to missionaries. The 'deep spirituality' of African church leaders was recognized. Joe Church, a medical missionary, reported on 'Times of refreshing in Ruanda'.[6] This revival movement, through its emphasis on brokenness in the Christian life, would affect Western evangelical spirituality, especially through the influence of Roy Hession and his book *The Calvary Road*. Festo Kivengere, a child of the East African Revival who became a bishop in Uganda, spoke at Keswick in 1972 and 1975.

In the decades after the Second World War, Keswick increasingly accepted that spirituality was linked with movements for justice. In 1949 Rachel John, a missionary in India who spoke to the Convention dressed in Indian costume, pointed out that new roles for women were emerging in the non-Western world. 'Many educated Indian women', she said, 'now take up church work as their vocation . . . some become teachers and doctors.' Eileen Barter Snow, a doctor who was the principal of the famous Christian Medical College at Ludhiana, gave Keswick more information about the Indian scene in her reports in the 1950s. She spoke of one Indian Christian girl who wanted to be a doctor but could not do so because to be accepted for training through government channels she had to sign a document saying that she was a Hindu. She was now being trained through a grant from a school in England. Snow argued for the good news to be demonstrated, concluding by stating that India's message to the West was: 'Don't talk of love; come and show it.'

The call to overseas mission has been sustained. George Verwer, the founder of Operation Mobilisation, brought a powerful challenge to the Convention. Verwer issued an impassioned plea to preach holiness and the Lordship of Christ. Mike Fitton, one of those who heard Verwer, had attended the missionary meeting feeling that it had little spiritual relevance to him. But when Verwer spoke of the needs of the world Fitton thought: 'Why don't enough people go?' Mike Fitton and his future wife, Gilly (whom he met that year in the tent at Keswick), both felt a call to mission. Their story of a sense of call coming at Keswick is typical of many others, right up to the present time. In 1993 Mike Fitton was badly injured during his work as a policeman and had to retire from the police force. The result was that he began a ministry with Crusaders in the north of England.[7] The call to mission, he realized, could be to mission in his home country.

Mission and motivation

The appeal to live life under Christ's Lordship, so frequently made at Keswick, logically leads to the call to mission and wholehearted discipleship. And we conclude this small book by returning to the issue of motivation that Paul addressed so clearly in his response to his critics in Corinth. His motivations were entirely based on his vision of Christ and his work.

First, we are loved by Jesus our Saviour. 'For Christ's love compels us, because we are convinced that one died for all' (2 Corinthians 5:14). The first reason for wholehearted service wherever God calls us is that we are loved. We are pushed forward in our work by the compulsion of Christ's love. And this is the logic of the gospel described by Paul in verses 14 and 15. As one translation puts it, *'The love of Christ leaves me no choice.'*

And so it has been for many called to mission around the world, or called to live a life of committed discipleship at home. It is our awareness that our life has been radically changed by God's love expressed in Christ, and that it is not solely for personal fulfilment. Christ died for all. He gave himself for us. He gave everything he had. So we no longer live for ourselves, but for him.

Tim Chester tells the story from the early twentieth century of Sister Eva of Friedenshort, who in 1905 told a meeting for ladies at Keswick how she had disposed of all her possessions to serve Christ. 'The only things she still had were a ring and clasp which she'd kept for sentimental reasons. But now the Lord was impressing upon her afresh the needs of the lost and so she laid them on the table at the front. One after another, women followed her example and put jewellery, watches and coins on the table.'[8]

Since Christ gave everything, we are called to respond to that sacrificial love in joyful surrender to him and to his good purposes. The first great incentive for our discipleship and mission, the first motivating force in Christian service of any kind, is that we are loved by Jesus our Saviour.

Second, we are responsible to Jesus our Judge. 'For we must all appear before the judgment seat of Christ' (2 Corinthians 5:10). Here Paul describes an important reminder of a future reality. He is describing a judgment that Christians will face. The judgment he describes is not a judgment concerning our eternal destiny. Rather, it will be a time for giving an account of how we have lived our life, a judgment on our stewardship. This verse is best understood when placed alongside Paul's teaching in his first letter to the Corinthians (3:11–15). He writes there of the importance of ensuring that our lives are built on the foundation of Christ. He is the one foundation, who will withstand all tests. We are secure if our lives are built on him. But there is more to be said. The question remains, how will we build on that foundation? Will we build with those things that are short-lived – wood, hay, straw – or will we build with those things that are of lasting

> *Since Christ gave everything, we are called to respond to that sacrificial love in joyful surrender to him and to his good purposes.*

value – gold, silver, precious stones? Because one day the quality of our building work will be tested, and on that judgment day will it survive or will it disappear in a cloud of smoke?

So how you build matters. How you live your life counts. That judgment day for Christians is not intended to cloud our hope or dampen our joy at the prospect of being with Christ. Rather, it is there as a stimulus to faithful service, a reminder of our obligation to live for Christ. How do I use my time, my gifts, my resources and the many God-given opportunities I have? All these things matter, Paul says, in the light of the future. Will we look back on our lives and see that we have built only things that are temporary, or will we have built something that will last, something for eternity? It's a stimulus to faithful service, a call to be wholehearted in living for the values of God's kingdom, not building for personal and therefore for temporary gain.

And, finally, we are sent by Jesus our King. 'We are therefore Christ's ambassadors, as though God were making his appeal through us. We implore you on Christ's behalf: Be reconciled to God' (2 Corinthians 5:20). Having been reconciled, I am now a minister of reconciliation. Paul uses the illustration of the ambassador, the king's envoy, and it is a bold analogy. As Paul implies, we are speaking on behalf of God. It is as though *God were making his appeal through us*! We are speaking *on Christ's behalf* (v. 20). It is not uncommon today, in a world of pluralistic religion and militant secularism, for Christians to be accused of arrogance in claiming that the gospel is for every person in every culture. What gives us the right? It's not unusual for us to hear: 'It's OK for you, but don't try to absolutize it. What right do you have to push your faith on others? It's all a matter of personal choice.'

These verses help us respond with conviction to such a question. Christians are called to proclaim that *Christ died for all*, and the basis of their authority is that they speak *on Christ's behalf.* We should never shrink from the task of Christian proclamation or be intimidated by today's religious pluralism. The ministry of reconciliation is founded on the fact that we are sent by the King. It has both authority and urgency: we implore on Christ's behalf.

As we have considered the priorities that continue to shape the Keswick movement, we have frequently underlined that they point to one person: Christ himself. It is his Lordship that we proclaim. It is his glory for which we long. It is his life we wish to live. And it is this Christ-centred vision that must continue to shape the Keswick movement. It is not a new strategy but a new inspiration. The apostle Paul has shown us that the basic motivation and inspiration is the Lord Jesus himself. We are loved by Jesus our Saviour, we are responsible to Jesus our Judge, we are sent by Jesus our King.

John Stott wrote about our Christian mission in this way:

Nothing is more important for the recovery of the church's mission (where it has been lost), or its development (where it is weak), than a fresh, clear and comprehensive vision of Jesus Christ. When he is demeaned, and especially when he is denied, in the fullness of his unique person and work, the church lacks motivation and direction, our morale crumbles and our mission disintegrates. But when we see Jesus, it is enough. We have all the inspiration, incentive, authority and power we need.

Epilogue

According to one ancient Chinese proverb, to prophesy is extremely difficult – especially with regard to the future! So it would be unwise to spend too long at the end of this small book outlining what we envision the future of the Keswick movement to be. When it began at the end of the nineteenth century, no-one could have anticipated its global reach or predicted its eternal outcomes, and neither can that be done today. Nevertheless, we sense that the priorities of the movement, which we have articulated in this book, are still needed in the evangelical world today – and tomorrow. Our core convictions can be summed up by four simple statements of priority.

First, hearing God's Word: the Scriptures are the foundation for the church's life, growth and mission, and we must remain committed to preaching and teaching God's Word in a way that is faithful to Scripture and relevant to Christians of all ages and backgrounds. There is no doubt that this must remain a core priority for the health and growth of God's church worldwide.

Second, becoming like God's Son: as we have seen, from its earliest days the Keswick movement has encouraged Christians to live godly lives in the power of the Spirit, and to grow in Christlikeness. We have underlined that this is God's will for his people in every culture and generation. There are many signals that suggest that, whilst evangelicals are concerned to engage with culture and to avoid pietistic withdrawal from the world, we are not giving our energies to equipping and encouraging God's people in the demanding task of genuine and distinct godliness We must continue to address this.

Third, serving God's mission: we have underlined that the authentic response to God's Word is obedience to his mission, and the inevitable result of Christlikeness is sacrificial service. We must continue to encourage committed discipleship in family life, work and society, and energetic engagement in the cause of world mission.

Fourth, uniting God's people: at a time when evangelicals have grown in numbers the world over, there are disturbing signs of growing fracture lines. Even among those who would affirm an evangelical statement of faith, new divisions are emerging on what might previously have been understood to be secondary matters. We long that the Keswick movement will sustain its gospel priorities and evangelical commitments, uniting Christians across the denominations, across generations, and across cultures around the core priorities of the movement.

If these priorities are to be maintained and extended, then there is no question that we are dependent upon God's grace and wisdom, and will need to see a new generation of women and men rise up to carry the work forward around the world. Just as the living God has equipped and energized his people over the past 140 years of the Keswick movement, so we can be sure that, according to his good purposes, he will do so again. May it be for the glory of Christ Jesus, the Lord!

Notes

Preface

1. Charles Price & Ian Randall, *Transforming Keswick* (Carlisle: OM Publishing, 2000).

1. Longing for God's blessing

1. D. A. Carson, *A Call to Spiritual Reformation* (Leicester: IVP, 1992), pp. 15, 16.
2. W. B. Sloan, *These Sixty Years: The Story of the Keswick Convention* (London: Pickering & Inglis, 1935), pp. 9–11.
3. Alexander Smellie, *Evan Henry Hopkins: A Memoir* (London: Marshall Bros., 1920), pp. 52–56.
4. H. W. Webb-Peploe, *The Life of Privilege* (New York: Nisbet & Co., 1896), pp. 64–69.
5. *Memoir of T. D. Harford-Battersby*, by two of his sons (London, 1890), p. 151.
6. *The Christian's Pathway of Power*, 1 September 1877, p. 177.
7. Handley Moule, F. B. Meyer, Hubert Brooke and Elder Cumming wrote a 'Manual of Keswick Teaching' in 1906, entitled *Holiness by Faith* (London: Religious Tract Society, 1906).
8. J. I. Packer, *Knowing God* (London: Hodder & Stoughton, 1973), p. 228.

2. Hearing God's Word

1. *The Life of Faith*, 1 September 1880, p. 162.
2. See Price and Randall, *Transforming Keswick*, pp. 41, 58.
3. J. R. W. Stott, *I Believe in Preaching* (London: Hodder & Stoughton, 1982), p. 126.
4. I have written more fully on this topic, using the Nehemiah account as a foundation, in Jonathan Lamb, *Preaching Matters: Encountering the Living God* (IVP / Keswick Ministries, 2014), pp. 41ff.
5. H.F. Stevenson, ed., *Keswick's Authentic Voice* (London: Marshall Morgan & Scott, 1959), p. 11.
6. George Duncan spoke at thirty-one Keswicks, a record number. See Price and Randall, *Transforming Keswick*, p. 78.
7. Tim Chester, *Mission Matters: Love Says Go* (IVP / Keswick Ministries, 2015).

3. Proclaiming God's gospel

1. Quoted in Peter Lewis, *The Message of the Living God*, Bible Speaks Today (IVP, 2000), pp. 19–20.
2. David Bebbington, *Evangelicalism in Modern Britain: A History from the 1730s to the 1980s* (London: Routledge, 1995), pp. 162–164.
3. Price and Randall, *Transforming Keswick*, p. 196, quoting from *The Mid-America Keswick Week*, 1959.
4. Jeremy and Elizabeth McQuoid, *The Amazing Cross* (IVP / Keswick Ministries, 2012).

4. Becoming like God's Son

1. John Stott, *The Last Word: Reflections on a Lifetime of Preaching* (Authentic Media, 2008), p. 19.

2. J. I. Packer, *Serving the People of God*, Collected Shorter Writings of J. I. Packer (Carlisle: Paternoster Press, 1998), p. 321.

3. For Newman see S. Gilley, *Newman and His Age* (London: DLT, 1990).

4. A. Smellie, *Evan Henry Hopkins: A Memoir* (London: Marshall Bros., 1921), p. 81; cf. Bebbington, *Evangelicalism in Modern Britain*, p. 173.

5. E. H. Hopkins, *The Law of Liberty in the Spiritual Life* (London: Marshall Bros., 1884) pp. 92–102.

6. For the influence of Scroggie see Ian Randall, *Evangelical Experiences* (Carlisle: Paternoster Press, 1999), chapter 2.

7. For Holden see M. Broomhall, *John Stuart Holden: A Book of Remembrance* (London: Hodder & Stoughton, 1935).

8. *The Keswick Week*, 1924, pp. 165–166.

9. *The Life of Faith*, 11 July 1951, p. 479.

10. Peter Maiden, *Discipleship Matters* (IVP/Keswick Foundations, 2015).

5. Depending on God's Spirit

1. *The Christian*, 19 February 1925, p. 15. F. B. Meyer was recalling his early experiences of Keswick.

2. S. Barabas, *So Great Salvation: The History and Message of the Keswick Convention* (London: Marshall, Morgan & Scott, 1952), p. 180.

3. Meyer, *A Keswick Experience/*, p. 3; *The Life of Faith*, 25 July 1928, p. 850.

4. *The Life of Faith*, 29 July 1903, p. 529.

5. *Bethesda Record*, July 1912, p. 115.

6. *The Life of Faith*, 12 August 1903, p. 572.

7. *The Keswick Week*, 1905, p. 56.

8. See John C. Pollock, *The Keswick Story* (Fort Washington, PA: CLC, 2006 revised edition), pp. 165–170.

9. J. B. Figgis, *Keswick from Within* (London: Marshall Bros., 1914), p. 151.
10. Cited in Robert Lescelius, 'Spurgeon and Revival', *Reformation and Revival*, vol. 3, no. 2 (Spring 1994).
11. Tim Chester, *Mission Matters: Love Says Go* (IVP/Keswick Ministries, 2015).

6. Uniting God's people

1. Pollock, *The Keswick Story*, p. 147.
2. *The Life of Faith*, 10 February 1926, p. 14; *The Baptist Times*, 21 July 1932, p. 513.
3. *The Christian*, 21 July 1938, p. 8.
4. *The Keswick Week*, 1910, p. 120.
5. *The Christian*, 5 February 1925, p. 6; 12 February 1925, pp. 20–22. See K. Hylson-Smith, *Evangelicals in the Church of England, 1734–1984* (Edinburgh: T & T Clark, 1989), p. 222.
6. *The Life of Faith*, 6 July 1921, p. 746. Randall, *Evangelical Experiences*, chapters 2 and 3.
7. W.B. Sloan, *These Sixty Years: The Story of the Keswick Convention* (London: Pickering & Inglis, 1935), p. 67.
8. George Duncan, 'To the ends of the earth', in John Caiger, et al., *100 Years of the Keswick Convention* (London: Keswick Convention, 1975), pp. 18–22.
9. Prince and Randall, *Transforming Keswick*, pp. 11–12.
10. Keswick Council, *The Keswick Convention: Platform Ministry of Women* (1999).

7. Seeking God's face

1. *The Life of Faith*, 1 September 1880, p. 162.
2. *The Life of Faith*, 1 September 1884, p. 167.
3. *The Life of Faith*, 1 July 1880, p. 127.

4. F. S. Webster, 'Keswick Hymns', in C. F. Harford, *The Keswick Convention: Its Message, Its Method and Its Men* (London: Marshall Bros., 1907), p. 214.

5. *The Keswick Week*, 1909, p. 91.

6. *The Christian*, 15 July 1920, pp. 1–2.

7. *The Witness*, August 1926, p. 394.

8. Minutes of the Keswick Council, 20 April 1928.

9. J. I. Packer, *Knowing God* (Hodder & Stoughton, 1973), p. 18.

10. *The Freeman*, 20 May 1887, p. 336.

11. Price and Randall, *Transforming Keswick*, p. 112.

12. Price and Randall, *Transforming Keswick*, p. 256.

8. Serving God's mission

1. E. Stock, *My Recollections* (London: James Nisbet & Co. Ltd., 1909), p. 203.

2. E. Stock, 'The Missionary Element', in C.F. Harford, ed., *The Keswick Convention: Its Message, Its Methods and Its Men*, pp. 135–136.

3. *The Life of Faith*, 21 September 1938, p. 975.

4. For Amy Carmichael see E. Elliot, *Amy Carmichael: Her Life and Legacy* (Eastbourne: MARC, 1988).

5. W. B. Sloan, *These Sixty Years: The Story of the Keswick Convention* (London: Pickering & Inglis, 1935), pp. 49–50.

6. See J. E. Church, *Quest for the Highest* (Exeter: Paternoster, 1981).

7. Report by Mike and Gilly Fitton submitted at Keswick, 1998.

8. Tim Chester, *Mission Matters: Love Says Go* (IVP / Keswick Ministries, 2015).

KESWICK MINISTRIES

Our purpose

Keswick Ministries is committed to the spiritual renewal
of God's people for his mission in the world.

God's purpose is to bring his blessing to all the nations
of the world. That promise of blessing, which touches
every aspect of human life, is ultimately fulfilled through
the life, death, resurrection, ascension and future return of
Christ. All of the people of God are called to participate in
his missionary purposes, wherever he may place them. The
central vision of *Keswick Ministries* is to see the people of
God equipped, encouraged and refreshed to fulfil that
calling, directed and guided by God's Word in the power
of his Spirit, for the glory of his Son.

Our priorities: *Keswick Ministries* seeks to serve the local
church through:

- **Hearing God's Word**: the Scriptures are the foundation
  for the church's life, growth and mission, and *Keswick
  Ministries* is committed to preach and teach God's Word
  in a way that is faithful to Scripture and relevant to
  Christians of all ages and backgrounds.
- **Becoming like God's Son**: from its earliest days the
  Keswick movement has encouraged Christians to live
  godly lives in the power of the Spirit, to grow in Christlikeness and to live under his lordship in every area of
  life. This is God's will for his people in every culture
  and generation.
- **Serving God's mission**: the authentic response to
  God's Word is obedience to his mission, and the
  inevitable result of Christ-likeness is sacrificial service.

Keswick Ministries seeks to encourage committed discipleship in family life, work and society, and energetic engagement in the cause of world mission.

Our ministry

- **Keswick: the event**. Every summer the town of Keswick hosts a three-week Convention, which attracts some 15,000 Christians from the UK and around the world. The event provides Bible teaching for all ages, vibrant worship, a sense of unity across generations and denominations, and an inspirational call to serve Christ in the world. It caters for children of all ages and has a strong youth and young adult programme. And it all takes place in the beautiful Lake District – a perfect setting for rest, recreation and refreshment.

- **Keswick: the movement**. For 140 years the work of Keswick has impacted churches worldwide, and today the movement is underway throughout the UK, as well as in many parts of Europe, Asia, North America, Australia, Africa and the Caribbean. *Keswick Ministries* is committed to strengthen the network in the UK and beyond, through prayer, news, pioneering and cooperative activity.

- **Keswick resources**. *Keswick Ministries* is producing a growing range of books and booklets based on the core foundations of Christian life and mission. It makes Bible teaching available through free access to mp3 downloads, and the sale of DVDs and CDs. It broadcasts online through Clayton TV and annual BBC Radio 4 services. In addition to the summer Convention, Keswick Ministries is hoping to develop other teaching and training events in the coming years.

Our unity

The Keswick movement worldwide has adopted a key Pauline statement to describe its gospel inclusivity: *'for you are all one in Christ Jesus'* (Galatians 3:28). *Keswick Ministries* works with evangelicals from a wide variety of church backgrounds, on the understanding that they share a commitment to the essential truths of the Christian faith as set out in our statement of belief.

Our contact details

Mail: Keswick Ministries, Keswick Convention Centre, Skiddaw Street, Keswick, CA12 4BY, England
T: 017687 80075
E: info@keswickministries.org
W: www: keswickministries.org

Knowing God Better

Five Keswick talks from John Stott, Jonathan Lamb, Paul Mallard, Ajith Fernando and Charles Price to enable you to know God better.

BARCODE: 5021776212140
2 DVD   SWP2121A

What are we made for? What is the purpose of our lives? What really matters? The answer is found in Paul's prayer: that you may know God better.

Bible teaching from five respected Keswick speakers has been carefully selected to create this unique DVD collection. With the accompanying book, Knowing God Better introduces the key priorities that shape the Keswick movement, priorities which are essential for every Christian who longs to know the living God.

Speakers and topics include:

John Stott – 'Becoming More Like Christ'

Jonathan Lamb – 'Saved by the triune God' (Ephesians 1:3-14)

Paul Mallard – 'Walking in the Spirit' (Galatians 5:13-26)

Charles Price – 'A transforming experience of God' (Isaiah 6)

Ajith Fernando – 'God's missionary heart' (Jonah 4)

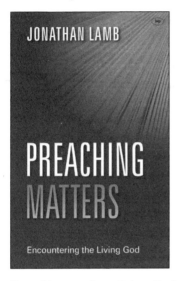

also by Jonathan Lamb

Preaching Matters

*Encountering
the Living God*
Jonathan Lamb

ISBN: 978-1-78359-149-7
192 pages, paperback

Preaching matters. It is a God-ordained means of encountering Christ. This is happening all around the world. The author recalls the student who, on hearing a sermon about new life in Christ, found faith which changed his life and future forever; and the couple facing the trauma of the wife's terminal illness who discovered that Christ was all they needed, following a sermon on Habakkuk.

When the Bible is faithfully and relevantly explained, it transforms hearts, understandings and attitudes, and, most of all, draws us into a living relationship with God through Christ.

This is a book to ignite our passion for preaching, whether we preach every week or have no idea how to put a sermon together. It will encourage every listener to participate in the dynamic event of God's Word speaking to his people through his Holy Spirit. God's Word is dynamite; little wonder that its effects are often dynamic.

'A book for both preachers and listeners … a fitting manifesto not just for the Keswick Convention, but for every local church.'
Tim Chester

Available from your local Christian bookshop or **www.thinkivp.com**

related titles from IVP

Mission Matters

Love says go
Tim Chester

ISBN: 978-1-78359-280-7
176 pages, paperback

The Father delights in his Son. This is the starting point of mission, its very core. The word 'mission' means 'sending'. But for many centuries this was only used to describe what God did, sending his Son and his Spirit into the world. World mission exists because the Father wants people to delight in his Son, and the Son wants people to delight in the Father.

Tim Chester introduces us to a cascade of love: love flowing from the Father to the Son through the Spirit. And that love overflows and, through us, keeps on flowing to our Christian community and beyond, to a needy world. Mission matters. This book is for ordinary individuals willing to step out and be part of the most amazing, exciting venture in the history of the world.

'If you want to fire up your church with a vision for global mission, this is your book! ... It should carry a spiritual health warning.'
David Coffey OBE

'I am sure this book will provoke many to respond to the challenge as they realize that there are still thousands waiting to be introduced to the Saviour.' Helen Roseveare

Available from your local Christian bookshop or **www.thinkivp.com**

related titles from IVP

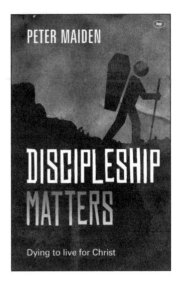

Discipleship Matters
Dying to live for Christ
Peter Maiden

ISBN: 978-1-78359-355-2
176 pages, paperback

Discipleship involves a gentle journey with our Saviour. Its demands will dovetail happily with our carefully crafted plans.

Wrong. Peter Maiden pulls no punches as he looks at what a disciple should look like today. Are we prepared to follow Jesus' example? Lose our lives for his sake? Live counter-culturally in a world that values power, prestige and money, and constantly puts self at the centre?

Of all people, Jesus, the Son of God, has the authority to require this of us. And he's calling us to a relationship, not to a set of rules or a miserable, spartan existence. In fact, it is through losing our lives that we find them, and thereby discover the source of pure joy.

What a pity we set the bar too low.

Available from your local Christian bookshop or **www.thinkivp.com**

related titles from IVP

KESWICK STUDY GUIDE 2015

The Whole of Life for Christ

Becoming everyday disciples

Antony Billington
& Mark Greene

ISBN: 978-1-78359-361-3
96 pages, booklet

Suppose for a moment that Jesus really is interested in every aspect of your life. Everything - the dishes and the dog and the day job and the drudgery of some of the stuff you just have to do, the TV programme you love, the staff in your local supermarket as well as the homeless in the local shelter, your boss as well as your vicar, helping a shopper find the ketchup as well as brewing the tea for the life group, the well-being of your town and the well-being of your neighbour

Suppose the truth that every Christian is a new creature in Christ, empowered by the Spirit to do his will, means that Christ is with you everywhere you go, in every task you do, with every person you meet ... Suppose God wants to involve you in what he's doing in the places you spend your time day by day ... Suppose your whole life is important to Christ ...

He does.

These seven studies will help you explore and live out the marvellous truth that the gospel is an invitation into whole-life discipleship, into a life following and imitating Jesus.

Available from your local Christian bookshop or **www.thinkivp.com**

JEREMY & ELIZABETH McQUOID

THE AMAZING CROSS

Transforming lives today

related titles from IVP

The Amazing Cross
Transforming lives today
Jeremy & Elizabeth
McQuoid

ISBN: 978-1-84474-587-6
192 pages, paperback

The cross of Christ is the heartbeat of Christianity. It is a place of pain and horror, wonder and beauty, all at the same time. It is the place where our sin collided gloriously with God's grace.

But do we really understand what the cross is all about? Or are we so caught up in the peripherals of the faith that we have forgotten the core? We need to ask ourselves:

- How deep an impact has the cross made on my personality?
- Do I live in the light of the freedom it has won for me?
- Am I dying to myself every day, so that I can live for Christ?
- Do I face suffering with faith and assurance?
- Can I face death in the light of the hope of the resurrection?

The authors present us with a contemporary challenge to place all of our lives, every thought, word and deed, under the shadow of the amazing cross, and allow that cross to transform us here and now.

'It is an ideal introduction to the heart of the Christian gospel, and a very welcome addition to the Keswick Foundation series.'
Jonathan Lamb

Keswick Study Guides by IVP

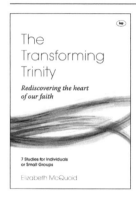

The Transforming Trinity
Rediscovering the heart of our faith
Elizabeth McQuoid

These seven studies will help you grow in your understanding of the inexhaustible riches of the Trinity. Find out why the Trinity is central to our beliefs and fundamental to the working out of our faith. Learn to worship the triune God more fully, reflect his image more clearly, and experience his transforming power in your life. Learn what it really means to know the Father, follow the Son, and walk in the Spirit. Because the Trinity is at the heart of Christian faith and life.

'A feast for individuals and Bible study groups.'
Sam Allberry

ISBN: 978-1-84474-906-5 | 80 pages, booklet

Really?
Searching for reality in a confusing world
Elizabeth McQuoid

These seven studies help us go deeper into the truth we are offered in Jesus Christ, and to root our lives in it. Because Jesus offers us himself, a reality that satisfies not only our intellectual curiosity, but also the deepest longings of our hearts. He offers us true security and sure hope for the future. He reshapes our thoughts, our life, our identity and our purpose. Real truth is found in Jesus Christ, and knowing him changes everything.

'Really? is a great resource to explore how the Christian message enables us to live with real confidence in the real world.' Tim Chester

ISBN: 978-1-78359-158-9 | 80 pages, booklet

Available from your local Christian bookshop or **www.thinkivp.com**